The Business of Tourism: Urban-led Growth?

Editors

Sheila Flanagan
and
Ciarán Conlon

BLACKHALL
Publishing

This book was typeset by Artwerk for

BLACKHALL PUBLISHING
26 Eustace Street
Dublin 2
Ireland

e-mail: blackhall@tinet.ie

© individual contributors, 1999

ISBN: 1 901657 43 4

A catalogue record for this book is available from the British Library.

Printed in Ireland by
ColourBooks Ltd.

CONTENTS

PROFILES OF CONTRIBUTORS

Louise Browne
Policy and Planning Manager, Northern Ireland Tourist Board
Louise works with the Northern Ireland Tourist Board based initially in the Board's Development Division. She has particular responsibility for development planning. Her role has recently expanded to include responsibility for wider aspects of tourism policy within the newly formed Policy and Planning Division.

Oliver Costello
Head of Commercial Activities and Deputy Manager, Aer Rianta
Oliver Costello's primary responsibility is for Aer Rianta's retail and concessionary activities at Dublin Airport. He is a Fellow of the Chartered Institute of Management Accountants and holds a MSc (Mgmt) and MBA degree from Trinity College, Dublin and Dublin City University respectively.

Dr Sheila Flanagan
Faculty of Tourism and Food, Dublin Institute of Technology, Dublin
Dr Flanagan is a lecturer in tourism policy and planning at Dublin Institute of Technology. She has carried out planning research for numerous local authorities and tourism agencies in Ireland, Poland and Finland and acts as technical advisor to the Federation of European City Tourist Offices.

John Higgins
Head of Secretariat, Western Development Commission
In 1995, John Higgins was appointed Chief Executive of the Western Development Partnership Board. This Board was appointed by the government to co-ordinate a response to the needs of the west of Ireland. This plan was presented to government and contained many innovative proposals for action including the replacement of the Western Development Partnership by a new Commission with significant terms of reference and with an investment fund of £100 million.

John Kelly
Head of Business Banking, AIB
John Kelly has worked primarily in lending related activities
with both corporate and retail customers. He was appointed
Head of Business Banking in December 1996 with overall
responsibility for shaping and implementing the Bank's policies
for business customers in Ireland.

Frank Magee
Chief Executive, Dublin Tourism
Frank Magee is also a member of the Board of the Federation of
European City Tourist Offices (FECTO) and the Chair of
Information Technology working Group of FECTO.

John Moreu
President, Federation of European City Tourist Offices
John Moreu is Managing Director of the Amsterdam Tourist
Office, which plays a central role in tourism in and around the
city. Tourism has become one of the principal elements of the
economy of the Amsterdam region.

Mark Mortell
Chairman, Bord Fáilte Éireann
Mark Mortell is also Chairman of the Overseas Tourism
Marketing Initiative since 1995. He is also Head of Marketing at
Bank of Ireland Lifetime.

Phil Reilly
Property Manager and Project Director, Monarch Properties
Monarch Properties has been involved in property development
in Ireland, the UK and USA for the past 25 years. It is involved in
a £25 million tourist and leisure development in Tralee which is
a joint venture with Tralee UDC.

Dr Roger Vaughan
**Department of Tourism and Retail Management, University of
Bournemouth**
Roger Vaughan is a Principal Lecturer at Bournemouth
University. He has extensive experience on the impact of tourism
in many areas.

ACKNOWLEDGEMENTS

Our thanks go first and foremost to the contributors whose presentations made the conference worthwhile.

The Conference was organised by the Tourism and Environment sub-committee of Dublin Chamber of Commerce whose enthusiasm and support was an important ingredient in its success. Laurence Crowley, Executive Chairman of the Michael Smurfit Business School kindly agreed to open the conference and Mark Mortell, Chairman Bord Fáilte presented the opening address.

A special word of thanks is due to those who chaired the various sessions: Mr John McNally (President Dublin Chamber of Commerce (1997-1998)), Paul Carty (Managing Partner Deloittle and Touche), Margaret Fleming (Head of Research, Jones, Lang Wooton), Brendan Leahy (Chief Executive, Irish Tourist Industry Confederation) and Professor James Crowley (Department of Business Administration, UCD).

To everybody in Dublin Chamber of Commerce who helped in the organisational and event management a very special word of thanks and finally a special word of gratitude is due to our sponsors – Aer Rianta, Allied Irish Banks Plc, Deloitte and Touche and Jury's Hotel Group.

Ciarán Conlon
Research Director
Dublin Chamber of Commerce

Sheila Flanagan
Faculty of Tourism and Food
Dublin Institute of Technology

FOREWORD:

THE BUSINESS OF TOURISM: URBAN-LED GROWTH?

The Dublin Chamber of Commerce has long acknowledged the huge impact the tourism industry makes to the regional and national economy. The performance of Irish tourism is well ahead of European and world averages. While overseas tourist visits to Ireland grew by 7 per cent in 1997, the World Tourism Organisation's reports for 1997 show increases of 3.2 per cent in arrivals in Europe and 2.9 per cent in the world. Dublin is one of the most rapidly growing city destinations in Europe, and tourism is now Dublin's highest growth industry. Tourism numbers have been growing at an annual average of about 10 per cent during the 1990s. Industry reports for 1998 show that this trend has continued, with the total number of visitors to the city almost reaching 3 million – three times the population of the city.

Tourists spent more than £500 million in Dublin in 1998. For each tourist pound spent in Dublin, 26p is spent in hotels and guesthouses, 19p in the shops, 35p in pubs and restaurants, 10p on transport, and the balance on entertainment, sightseeing and other activities. Almost half of every pound spent by a tourist in Ireland reverts back to the central exchequer, or put another way more than £1 billion in tax revenue is generated by the industry over the year. All told, this spending supports about 26,000 jobs in Dublin's hotels, shops, restaurants and museums. In fact one in three new jobs created in Ireland since 1988 has been in the tourism sector.

The scale of the industry and its expansion over a 10-year period leaves much scope for analysis and review. In recognition of the remarkable performance by the sector over the last decade it was decided to bring together some central figures in the industry to see how best the growth could be sustained and managed.

This volume contains the proceedings of the first Dublin Chamber of Commerce Tourism Conference 'The Business of Tourism: Urban Led Growth?' held in The Michael Smurfit Graduate Business School, UCD on 4 April 1997. A deliberate attempt was made to organise the conference around a topical theme that would be of both industry and academic interest. The conference, of which these essays are the proceedings, was held to consider the opportunities that the growth of tourism offers to urban environments. It sought to analyse examples of successful experience both in Ireland (north and south) and Europe and to examine what the problems are and what needs to be done in order to make tourism work.

The first chapters in this volume outline the international and regional nature of urban tourism. Among the issues investigated are the character and extent of investment in the development of the urban product in Dublin and Amsterdam and the impact of air access through greater competition on UK and European routes, and partial deregulation on the transatlantic route. A number of intermediary, regionally-oriented organisations have emerged as vehicles for development and the issue of regionality and tourism has been the subject of much debate. A number of chapters describe the issues that must be faced in order to address these challenges.

Investment in tourism is growing rapidly and the sector's image is now one of professionalism and growth. The strategy for ensuring success and the implications for regeneration are the subject of the subsequent chapters.

Looking to the future, it will be clear from this volume that urban tourism is not the easy solution to the problems facing urban areas. It presents real opportunities. Future growth potential is likely to hinge on issues including the plans for the development of an international convention centre scheduled to be located in the city's docklands area, which is currently undergoing a major urban regeneration programme.

Sports-related tourism has also been identified as an area in which Dublin has considerable potential for growth. Successful events which took place in 1998 included the opening stages of the Tour de France in July, the Cutty Sark Tall Ships race in August and the Smurfit European Golf Open at the K Club, also in August. The Tall Ships event attracted over 1 million visitors to Dublin's quaysides and bay, while television coverage of the Tour de France is estimated to have attracted over 90 million viewers worldwide. Ireland has secured the hosting of the Ryder Cup in golf in 2005, and Dublin will host the Special Olympic Games in 2003. Dublin's sports infrastructure needs considerable improvement, however, if Dublin is to exploit its potential to attract international sports events. Many proposed developments are being considered, from a national stadium to a

50-metre swimming pool. When these facilities are available Ireland's, and Dublin's, capacity to attract major events will be significantly enhanced.

These issues are possibly material for debate for future conferences.

From all of the above it can be clearly seen that tourism is a business of vital concern to the national and regional economy. How that sector can continue to grow and sustain valuable jobs across the country was the focus of our conference. The business of tourism is a pervasive one and a lucrative one. Managing the success is the challenge facing us now. If we can get the correct balance in our policy going forward then the industry can continue to create jobs and income for many years to come.

Ciarán Conlon   Sheila Flanagan
Research Director   Faculty of Tourism and Food
Dublin Chamber of Commerce Dublin Institute of Technology

ADDRESS BY THE CHAIRMAN OF BORD FÁILTE,
MR MARK MORTELL TO THE DUBLIN CHAMBER OF
COMMERCE CONFERENCE

'THE BUSINESS OF TOURISM: URBAN-LED GROWTH?'

What do we mean by the concept of 'urban-led growth'? Does it mean, for instance, that urban settings – cities in particular – by virtue of their population density and consequent high level of facilities within a smaller area, automatically attract the tourism client in increasing numbers at the expense of the industry in the rural hinterland? Or does it mean that the tourism business interests in the urban setting actually set out to ensure that this is the case? Should we consider the Irish urban destinations in the same way that London, Paris or Amsterdam are known as free-standing destinations in their own right?

The fact that in the Irish context Dublin leads – indeed has always led – the rest of the country both in terms of international tourism numbers and revenue, will hardly come as a surprise to anyone. As the major point of air and sea access, as well as having all of the advantages which a historic capital city can offer combined with a new found cosmopolitan appeal (not to mention the regularity with which it hosts important international sporting fixtures), Dublin is likely to continue in this vein for the foreseeable future. But this is hardly the point. The real question is whether or not this welcome, growing success is happening at the expense – and by that I mean at the loss – of business in other regions of the country. Our international tourism figures are reflecting annual growth on a nationwide basis, and that trend is also economically forecast to continue well into the new century. Furthermore, the drive for growth on a nationwide basis is the principle upon which our national tourism policy for the future has been built.

While each individual sector within the industry understandably works to the benefit of its own business and that of its immediate location, it is by no means confined to urban areas. What is important to remember, however, is the fact that, as a direct result of the tourism policies that have been agreed between the government, Bord Fáilte and the various representative bodies from the tourism private sector, a new understanding of the need for partnership endeavour is now very much in evidence within the industry throughout the country.

Can any Irish, urban, tourism location, and Dublin in particular, be considered in the same way as London, Paris or New York, i.e. free-standing mass destinations in their own right with little or no reference to the appeal of the rest of their respective countries? While we may have recently noted in surveys that Dublin is now the second most popular short-break destination with British visitors, after Paris, and that such major attractions, such as Eurovision, international rugby and soccer matches, the new appeal of our film and music industries, and so on, all contribute to the growing success of the capital as a quality international destination in itself, tourism to Dublin in the main has a 'spin off' for the rest of the country.

If our successful national tourism growth, a growth which we fully expect to continue well into the new century, is in fact an urban-led phenomenon from which every region and district has potential to expand, then does it really matter in the end?

TOURISM IN DUBLIN: RECENT TRENDS AND FUTURE PROSPECTS

Frank Magee

Chief Executive
Dublin Tourism

INTRODUCTION

Dublin is recognised as one of the fastest-growing urban tourism destinations in Western Europe. Since 1988, Dublin has undergone a huge increase in visitor numbers and spend which has been consistent on an ongoing basis. Dublin has the longest length of stay by comparison with other European cities. The average European length of stay in a city is 2.5 nights, whilst in Dublin the figure is 6.5 nights. The city also has the highest level of room occupancy in Europe (See Table 1.1). This chapter examines the scale of these increases and the factors, which influenced the growth. Future prospects for tourism in Dublin are also addressed.

HISTORICAL BACKGROUND

1991 saw the formation of the new Dublin Tourism Regional Authority Ltd. Dublin Tourism, as an entity, took on responsibility for tourism development and marketing in the city and county of Dublin for the first time. Prior to 1991, Dublin Tourism had no marketing function. 1991 also coincided with the launch and first full year of the first operational programme for tourism funded by the European Regional Development Fund (ERDF). For analytical purpose it is a suitable base year as prior to 1991 statistics were compiled for a different geographical area.

Bord Fáilte and Central Statistic Office figures (Table 1.1) show the growth trend, which has occurred in Dublin in the area of visitor numbers and revenue since the base year of 1991.

Table 1.1: Growth Trends in Dublin

Year	Total Approved Rooms	Total Visitor Numbers (000s)	Visitor Revenue (IR£1m)
1991	8,220	1,379	242.6
1992	8,767	1,531	236.1
1993	9,308	1,693	313.8
1994	11,137	1,878	350.3
1995	13,000	2,264	439.8
1996	13,731	2,500 (est.)	475 (est.)

Source: Dublin Tourism

THE FACTORS OF CHANGE

A number of factors, including regional reorganisation, have influenced the success of tourism in Dublin.

The success of the millennium and European City of Culture in generating positive editorial and high-quality features on Dublin, in the international press, cannot be underestimated. The attraction of Dublin as a getaway place for film stars and the ensuing publicity from the success of films such as *The Commitments*, *My Left Foot* and *Michael Collins* have generated an interest in Dublin and made it a chic destination. This has been complemented by the success of U2, Boyzone, Chris de Burgh, Seamus Heaney and Maeve Binchy among others.

In 1991, Bord Fáilte supported the idea of promoting Dublin as a short-break destination. Bord Fáilte succeeded in getting carriers in twelve different destinations to include Dublin in their city breaks brochures. Samvinn Travel from Iceland worked with Dublin Tourism on developing a series of charters from Iceland to Dublin. The retail sector agreed to contribute towards a specific promotion that would have direct benefits for the trade. The role of retailers in contributing to marketing has continued to increase, however, when one looks at the real beneficiaries of tourism, it is argued that the retail sector should still be playing a much greater role in the marketing of Dublin.

The Dublin Cultural Connection was established as a co-operative marketing group of ten significant day visitor attractions by Dublin Tourism.

The biggest impact of all was the liberalisation of the air routes. Firstly, Ryanair played a huge role in lowering the cost and frequency of air transport and secondly, as a result of a change in government policy, direct flights to and from the USA were permitted. The change in traffic through Dublin Airport is charted in Table 1.2

Table 1.2 Traffic Flows through Dublin Airport 1991-1996

Year	Dublin Airport (000s)
1991	5,278
1992	5,808
1993	5,938
1994	6,980
1995	8,024
1996	9,091

Source: Aer Rianta

On sea routes, the HSS was introduced and the *Isle of Inismore* replaced the *Isle of Inisfree*. This resulted in faster, more frequent and more comfortable access by sea to Dublin.

Table 1.3: Sea Traffic Flow Change 1991-1996

	Irish Ferries	Stena
1991	100% (1.9 million)	100%
1996	137% (2.6 million)	139%

In addition to these factors, Dublin continues to experience a programme of extensive and attractive urban renewal. This has been complemented by the pedestrianisation of streets and the floodlighting of significant buildings.

Tourism has become the fastest growing job creator in Dublin's economy. The workforce has become much better educated and has benefited from extensive travel. One of the benefits of this travel is reflected in the growing number of high-quality restaurants catering for all budget ranges in Dublin.

PROFILE OF VISITORS

Market

The number of overseas tourists staying in Dublin for more than one night since 1991 has grown by 63 per cent. The average annual growth rate is 11.5 per cent. The domestic and Northern Irish market has not performed well when compared with other markets. One of the possible reasons for this was the perceived difficulty in securing accommodation in Dublin and also the fact that with increased demand the prices rose at a higher level in percentage terms than in other Irish destinations. Another, probably more significant factor, is the booming economy. Just as Ireland has become more accessible from the markets so those markets have become more accessible for the Irish. The cost of access to and from Dublin has been significantly reduced. This has resulted in a very large uptake in the number of Irish people going abroad on short-breaks.

Britain is the biggest market to Dublin accounting for 45 per cent of all overseas visitors and mainland Europe is second accounting for 30 per cent. North America accounts for 19 per cent. Mainland Europeans are the biggest spenders accounting for 41 per cent and British account for 20 per cent. One of the reasons for the variation between the British and the Europeans is because of the fact that the Europeans stay for a longer length of time.

Reason for Visit and Visitor Expenditure

Forty-nine per cent of all tourists come to Dublin during the months of June to September, however there is an anomaly where the quietest month for 4-star and 5-star hotel accommodation is August. One third of tourists arrive between October and March.

The main reason for visiting Dublin is for business or conference. If the city appears attractive to conference delegates and business travellers, they will prolong the length of their stay and will more than likely be well disposed to being accompanied by a travelling partner. Half of all visitors to Dublin are holidaymakers.

Dublin has the highest usage of hotels in the country, with 37 per cent of all tourists using hotels. Preliminary figures for 1996 show that the hotel sector has gained further market share. Dublin hotels also have the highest level of room occupancy in Europe and much of the credit for this must go to hotel groups, including Doyle Hotels and Jury's, which have large marketing departments and budgets.

Accommodation Growth

The growth in the accommodation base is not confined to the hotel sector as can be seen from Table 1.4 below which shows the changes in accommodation type between 1993 and 1996.

Table 1.4: Changes in Accommodation Type 1993-1996

Type	1993	1996	Increase (%)
Hotels	5,096	7,409	45
Guest Houses			
Irish Homes	1,715	2,252	31
Hostels	579	979	69
Caravan and Camping	272	550	102
Self-catering	307	384	25

Source: Dublin Tourism

There has been a phenomenal growth in the number of hotels in Dublin. During 1996 there was little difficulty in securing accommodation in Dublin, for the 1 million plus callers to the offices of Dublin Tourism. Between 1996 and 1999 there will be an increase of 114 per cent in the number of rooms available in Dublin. Trade indications are quite confident about the 1997 season and for future years.

FUTURE CHALLENGES

There is a serious danger for those new arrivals in the tourism sector who have little knowledge about how the market works and what is needed for long-term survival. The tourism distribution mechanism is a complex one, with very many intermediaries and one that requires a lead-in time to develop relationships with distributors. Another factor that new entrants need to realise is that tourists do not come to any particular destination because of a particular hotel. Therefore, these new entrants should be working to complement the efforts of the overall tourism product. The growth in the accommodation sector has not been confined to the hotel sector. This growth will continue to be evenly spread across all sectors of the trade.

If Dublin is to continue to increase its market share, Dublin

Tourism estimate that an additional £1 million a year must to be spent on marketing. This marketing effort should promote Dublin as a destination and should complement Tourism Brand Ireland.

Dublin is currently catching up on lost opportunities. When comparisons are made with other European cities, Dublin is lacking in the number of hotels available. Up until the arrival of the Conrad Group, the only international group in the city was Forte, new arrivals include Holiday Inn, Stakis and the Hilton.

Dublin's capacity to increase tourism, without it having a negative impact on tourism is a topical issue. Dublin Tourism believe that capacity exists to continue to increase the number of tourists without having an adverse effect on the experience. The trend to develop hotels on the periphery (the Naas Road, Tallaght, Dublin Airport, etc.) is a welcome one first identified in the Dublin Tourism 1990 Development Plan. The improved road network make the 45 golf courses in Dublin more accessible and the development of the Marina at Malahide will ultimately help tourism grow.

In the climate of globalisation, a factor in itself that can have a negative impact on tourism, is the effect that recent trends in retailing in Dublin will have on the visitor. As a result of the large increase in the number of British retailers in Dublin, we are in danger of loosing our distinct Irish identity. There is little that we can do about this, however that there is potential for those native stores to maximise the Irishness of their product by more effective marketing. If we look at where the average tourist pound is spent, the significance of this becomes apparent.

Market research shows that visitors to Dublin come for the atmosphere and the personal contact that is Dublin. Recent developments, which have succeeded in enhancing the visitors experience, include projects such as the Museum of Modern Art, Dublinia, The Dublin Writer's Museum and the James Joyce Cultural Centre. Day-visitor attractions, in future, must have a meaningful relationship with the Dublin experience. In this regard, the Smithfield Centre and the docks area will have the positive impact of spreading the numbers of visitors across a greater area and reducing the congestion that at times exists in areas such as Temple Bar and Grafton Street.

The litter situation must be tackled seriously otherwise Dublin's dirty image will impact negatively on the potential to attract additional visitors. Current tolerance of dirt is not confined to streets but extends to our buses and taxis. This area must be addressed by the Director of Traffic as part of his brief.

The advent of EMU and the further integration into Europe will result, not only in a harmonisation of currency and, ultimately, reduced costs, but will also impact negatively on the foreign experience, part of which is using foreign currency.

CONCLUSION

Providing Dublin can continue to satisfy visitors' needs and make people feel welcome, the city is well on the path to maintaining its position as one of the most important urban tourism destinations in Europe. Tourism in Dublin will continue to provide an increasing number of new full-time rewarding jobs and contribute to the economic well-being of Dublin.

TOURISM IN BELFAST: RECENT TRENDS AND FUTURE PROSPECTS

Louise Browne

Northern Ireland Tourist Board

INTRODUCTION

Until recently, the theme of urban tourism has not had its fair share of attention, with researchers and others tending to neglect the tourism function of the city. This neglect may be partly attributable to the fact that the impacts of tourism are often overshadowed by the impacts of other activities, especially in cities where change is the norm rather than the exception. The nature of tourism may indeed contribute to its low profile in the city. Yet the incremental impacts of tourism can be significant. These impacts will no doubt be illustrated by other contributions to this book. With particular reference to Belfast, while urban tourism has only recently become the subject of investigation, it is clear that tourism can represent a significant urban function and urban tourism is a topic worthy of considerably more attention.

OVERVIEW

This chapter provides a brief chronology of regeneration in Belfast and highlights the role that tourism plays through an examination of the role of tourism within the broader economic development strategy for the city. Future prospects for the development of urban tourism in Belfast are also considered.

REGENERATION IN BELFAST

When British troops arrived on the streets of Belfast in 1969, no one could have imagined that they would still be there some 29 years later. The view at the time was that the problem was short-term. However, the scale of violence increased dramatically in the years that followed. In 1972, the situation of direct rule from London, which was accompanied by a reorganisation of local government, left local authorities bereft of their housing, education and physical planning functions. By the early-1980s, Belfast had been brought to its knees economically, socially and physically. The city centre had become a major target for IRA bombing campaigns. Over the period 1969-1987 there were some 2,291 explosions in Belfast, 50 per cent of which were directed at shops and offices. As one commentator put it, "the prevailing image was one of a deranged city, driven made by self-inflicted wounds, its condition exacerbated by economic decline and political hopelessness".

This serves to highlight the point that, while Belfast may not be alone in its attempts to regenerate its economy using means broadly similar to those which have been employed in cities elsewhere, in Belfast regeneration is aimed at redressing the image of a city battered by unending violence and trying to resolve a seemingly intractable political problem. The mobilisation of economic and physical development in both urban and rural areas has been identified as a way of resolving the problem. Improvement in the quality of people's lives is seen as a precondition for greater equality, democracy and achievement of the elusive 'settlement'.

At a very early stage the crucial connection was made between economic development and management of the political process. It is a connection that continues to be reinforced not only by central government, but also by the EU through its structural funds and by the USA through the creation of the International Fund for Ireland with its emphasis on "economic and social advancement, contact, dialogue and reconciliation". It is this connection between economic development and management of the political process which has not only underpinned the regeneration of Belfast, but which sets the city apart.

In the 1970s, the focus was very much on housing renewal and the identification of Belfast Areas of Need. The newly created Northern Ireland Housing Executive assumed responsibility for housing province-wide – huge strides were made. This work was given further impetus by the Integrated Development Operations initiative, which was launched by the European Commission, and which saw Belfast vying with Naples for the title of most deprived city within the Community at that juncture.

The decision, taken in 1985, to prepare a new plan for the Belfast Urban Area was to signal a new departure – an attempt as the then Economy Minister, Richard Needham, stated "to provide a blueprint for strategic development…and at its core the reconstruction of Belfast city centre". "From the seventies," he continued, "when the city was dead, ringed by steel fences on the inside and the army on the outside, Belfast is now revitalised, coming to life with the arrival of 'High Street' stores" (Northern Ireland Information Service, 14 February 1990).

The stimulation of retail and office development in the city centre was coupled with a policy of restraint elsewhere in the Belfast Urban Area (Belfast Urban Area Plan 2001). Shopping and office development strategies were designed to strengthen the city centre base and counteract tendencies towards decentralisation. The public sector's role in facilitating private sector development in the central area was achieved through a variety of urban renewal measures – comprehensive development schemes, environmental works, infrastructure investment and improvements in access, parking and servicing. The key mechanism, however, in implementing policy was the Urban Development Grant. First introduced in 1982, Urban Development Grants were specifically aimed at city centre schemes and included funding for projects in the retail, office and entertainment sectors. By 1989, 3,561 applications had been received and £42.9 million paid out. Within the general sphere of commercial expansion, a few projects can be singled out as flagships of the regeneration effort. One such is Castlecourt, a £75 million shopping centre which attracted a significant Urban Development Grant. Castlecourt has generated some 1,800 jobs and occupies a key site in Belfast city centre accommodating 325,000 square feet of retail space, offices and parking spaces for 1,500 cars.

The opening of Castlecourt in April 1990 marked the peak of retail expansion in Belfast. In contrast to the retail and office sectors, the attack on regenerating inner city industry was less successful. A key mechanism was the Enterprise Zone. The Belfast Enterprise Zone was designated in 1981 along with similar zones elsewhere in the UK. It set out to test how far private sector activity could be encouraged to tackle the problems of urban decay, physical dereliction and economic decline of the inner city. Financial incentives in the form of rates relief and tax allowances together with reduced statutory and administrative controls combined to create an environment attractive to the private sector. There was a low net increase in job creation with jobs already in the zone constituting a high proportion of total jobs. The decision by government not to continue with the experiment testifies to the limits on its effectiveness.

The Laganside represents a major programme of development of more than 120 acres of land on both sides of the River Lagan adjacent to the city centre and Belfast inner harbour. It is providing the city with important environmental and recreational benefits as well as major infrastructure improvements with road and rail links.

It is important to note that throughout the late-1980s and into the early-1990s attempts to lever private investment for capital development as a mechanism for regeneration were supplemented by a focus on "multiple deprivation" which saw the adoption of targeting social need as an instrument of government policy. This was a realisation of the need not only to adopt a holistic approach to regeneration but to maintain a sense of community, and indeed a sense of communities, a key requirement to the sustainability of the city.

TOURISM IN BELFAST

Tourism policies cannot be considered in isolation from economic development policies of which they are a part and which, together with physical planning policies, have combined to give expression to the regeneration of the city. Any expansion of tourism is likely to make a contribution to economic growth as long as it does not displace similar activities. Tourism features highly as a component of economic policy because of its perceived capacity to generate local incomes. Indeed, it goes further than this. Investment for tourism involves the development of facilities, activities, physical environments and infrastructure which have benefits for local communities. It also involves marketing the city and selling an image which can assist in the attraction of industrial and commercial activities.

The first tourism plan for Belfast, the Greater Belfast Tourism Development Plan, was produced in 1987. Prepared for the Northern Ireland Tourist Board, the whole purpose of the strategy was to direct projects, programmes, promotion and marketing towards stimulating additional demand so as to create an

environment which was more favourable to private sector investment. From the tourism strategy framework, a tourism action
programme was detailed over a 5-year period with successful
implementation of this integrated programme requiring a partnership arrangement between the Department of Economic
Development, the Department of the Environment, the
Department of Education, the Tourist Board and the six local
authorities of Greater Belfast.

At the time of preparation of the strategy, tourist trips to
Greater Belfast made up 29 per cent of the total Northern Ireland
figure and accounted for 31 per cent of expenditure. The average
length of stay in the area was 5.5 days. To set Greater Belfast
tourism in the context of other UK cities, Table 2.1 illustrates the
main purpose of tourist trips to Greater Glasgow, a traditional
industrial city similar to Belfast, and the city of Edinburgh, a
recognised major tourist destination. There were certain similar-
ities between Glasgow and Belfast, neither city being regarded as
a traditional holiday destination. Glasgow has made huge strides
since then towards establishing a holiday market. Business plays
a major role in drawing visitors to all three cities. The main difference is the proportion of pure holidaymakers, as opposed to
persons visiting friends and relatives. Forty per cent of trips to
Edinburgh fall into the former category, compared with 18 per
cent for Greater Glasgow and 1 per cent for Greater Belfast.

Table 2.1: Main Purpose of Trip (1984)

	Greater Belfast	Greater Glasgow	Greater Edinburgh
Holiday	1%	18%	40%
Visiting Friends &			
Relatives	54%	44%	32%
Business	41%	35%	27%
Other	4%	3%	1%

Putting Belfast's performance within the context of Northern
Ireland tourism, Table 2.2 illustrates that the city does not play
the role one might expect of a 'capital', albeit a provincial one.
(The figures are based on a three year average 1991-1993.)

Table 2.2: Visitor Profile: Belfast

	Out of State Visitors	Domestic Visitors	Total
Trips	320,000 (26% NI)	20,000 (3% NI)	340,000 (16% NI)
Nights	1,810,000 (23% NI)	40,000 (1.5% NI)	1,850,000 (18% NI)
Spend	£44 million (25% NI)	£1 million (2% NI)	£45 million (20% NI)

Belfast generates one quarter of Northern Ireland's out-of-state visitor trade. It is neither a primary nor a secondary destination for the domestic holiday market, and it attracts a very small proportion of Republic of Ireland trade.

FUNDING OF TOURISM INITIATIVES

Nevertheless, since the early-1990s, the case for using tourism to promote economic development has been pursued from a number of angles and has availed of financial support from a number of sources. The Northern Ireland Tourist Board, for example, administers a scheme of selective financial assistance (Tourism Development Scheme) which has provided support for hotels, conference facilities, self-catering accommodation, bed and breakfast accommodation and youth hostels. It has also assisted public sector projects from tourist information centres to full scale visitor attractions. The Board also administers EU structural funds through the Tourism Sub-Programme 1994-1999, and in conjunction with our colleagues in the South, the International Fund for Ireland's Tourism Programme. More recently, under the Local Government (Miscellaneous Provisions) NI Order 1992, local authorities were provided with the means to specifically promote economic development. The Department of the Environment Circular LG/44/92 outlined a variety of activities which councils could adopt in order to promote economic development. Some examples include:

- developing strategies for economic regeneration;

- researching opportunities for sectors of industry, including tourism, in the area;

- purchasing land for industrial or commercial use;

- encouraging local companies to develop the necessary skills to attain the quality standards required to supply goods and services to councils;

- preparing professional publicity material to promote the area as a location for industry.

Although the economic initiatives which councils have pursued have differed between councils, of particular interest to most have been:

- encouraging the formation and expansion of the business sector in the community;
- promoting the development of tourism;
- encouraging inward investment;
- promoting cross community links.

Belfast City Council's first major initiative in the area was to organise and host the 1993 "Vision Conference" out of which emerged the key recommendation of the need to prepare a co-ordinated and coherent economic strategy for Belfast. The Council has taken a lead role in this and has created a new department with responsibility for economic development which is now the new home, not only for the Council's tourism endeavours, but also significantly for its arts and cultural activities. The economic development strategy commits the Council to "re-establishing Belfast as a prosperous, vibrant, attractive city in which to live, work, visit and do business". In 1995, the Council commissioned the preparation of a Belfast Tourism Strategy, supported by a steering group comprising Belfast Development Office, Laganside, Belfast Chamber of Commerce and Trade and the Northern Ireland Tourist Board.

1995 also witnessed the arrival of "peace". The eighteen months of the ceasefires provided a rare opportunity to glimpse the potential tourism market which Northern Ireland could attain in the absence of violence and political instability. In 1995 alone, the level of visits to Northern Ireland increased by 20 per cent.

Particularly encouraging was the large increase in holiday visits which grew by 67 per cent to account for 461,000 or 30 per cent of total visits. The overall occupancy rate in 1995 was the highest recorded in the last twenty years. The Northern Ireland Tourist Board Corporate Plan for the period 1995-1998 expected

Northern Ireland to move towards being a more mature visitor destination and begin to show similar characteristics to those of competitor regions. We expected the number of pure holiday visitors to double by 1998 (to 550,000) and then to represent around 30 per cent of all visitors. These targets supported a high level of aspiration for Belfast by the year 2000, as it was apparent from this period that there was strong latent demand for tourism to Northern Ireland, particularly from the Republic, and a willingness amongst operators to respond to a stronger demand. One of the central points to emerge was that the potential of the Belfast tourism economy was not confined to the attractiveness of Belfast but to the attractiveness of Northern Ireland and Ireland as a destination.

The twin ceasefires not only led to a considerable increase in visitor numbers in 1995, they also changed the context for investment. A report by Horwath and Horwath, published in February 1995 and based on analysis during the last months of the ceasefires, suggested that the demand for hotel bedrooms in Greater Belfast, defined as a 10-mile radius from the city centre, might be expected to grow by 16 per cent a year over the period 1994-2000, and that the number of hotel bedrooms (then 1,320 in 25 hotels) would need to double to accommodate the increase in demand.

Since the Horwath report, two more hotels have been completed – the Holiday Inn Express (2-star, 114 rooms) and Madisons (2-star, 34 rooms). A further five hotels are on site including the Hilton (4-star, 180 rooms) at Laganside, and Jury's Inn (2-star, 190 rooms) in Great Victoria Street.

Tourist numbers fell during the breakdown of the ceasefires between 1996-July 1998. It is calculated that the number of holiday visitors rose by 50 per cent in 1995 purely due to the ceasefires, but that all of this boost was lost in 1996. Although the number of holiday visitors is predicted to be higher in 1996 than in 1994, this increase is almost exactly in line with the pre-ceasefire growth rates and is thus unlikely to represent any residual effect of the ceasefires. Similar calculations indicate that the ceasefires had no positive impact on numbers of business visitors in 1995.

Today, though somewhat trapped politically and culturally between Dublin and London, Belfast has neither the romance of the former nor the big city buzz of the latter. It has a healthy mistrust of the car and yet it is one of the easiest cities to negotiate on wheels. It has made a virtue out of necessity – the "ring of steel", the security cordon, which isolated the city centre from the rest of Belfast and created a pedestrianised zone – no doubt contributed to its survival and commercial rejuvenation. Belfast, through different stages of regeneration, from housing renewal, to targeting social need, to commercial revitalisation, has laid secure foundations for a city "in which to live, work, visit and do business".

URBAN TOURISM:
THE EUROPEAN EXPERIENCE

John E Moreu

INTRODUCTION

European city tourism can be considered as the original form of tourism: think of the Romans, visiting cities for leisure purposes. And what about the 'Grand Tour' along Europe's cultural high-lights back in the 18th century? But in the middle of the 20th century, the role of the European cities in tourism was over-shadowed by the new upcoming trends: seaside holidays, active holidays, camping and others. However, if we look in a proper way to today's balance, cities are once again leading: better economics allow the client within Europe to take a second or a third short holiday or short break. Also, better connections allow long haul passengers to visit Europe more frequently.

WHY IS THIS SO IMPORTANT?

- City tourism creates year-round business to a city.

- It influences the local and regional economy considerably, although it is not always recognised in that way (it is not considered as a single industry).

- City tourism can not be considered as just another type of short break. It supports local quality of life (theatre, going out, shopping, attractions).

City tourism is a separate segment, with its own characteristics. For example: in Holland general tourism in the country went down last year by 1 per cent, whereas in Amsterdam it went up by almost 10 per cent and for Holland, Germany is the number one market. For Amsterdam, the UK, followed by the USA: a totally different market.

The past fifteen years have not been too bad for Amsterdam's tourist industry. However, it must be said that some of our competitors have done considerably better.

The declining competitive position of Amsterdam was reason enough for us to conduct a thorough study of the situation. A city like Amsterdam needs to remain within the European Top 10. Once you fall out of the ranking, you run the risk of being scratched off the list of potential clients, so increasing the chance of a downward spiral into oblivion.

To judge the effects of such a development on a city like Amsterdam, it's good to realise that tourism holds an undeniably important social-economic position. Annual turnover in Amsterdam amounts to almost 2 billion guilders and the tourist industry accounts for 50,000 jobs in Amsterdam and the surrounding area. Political interests are also at stake where tourism is concerned, seen from the perspective of job opportunities and the offering of high-quality cultural facilities.

To regain its market position, Amsterdam needed a new marketing strategy. In 1993 we performed three studies to support our new strategic marketing plan. Firstly, research into the composition of the current Amsterdam tourist visitor; secondly, a study of how Amsterdam is perceived by its visitors and finally, an analysis of Amsterdam compared to its ten most important European competitors.

This latter study offered us a wealth of information which can also be of use to other tourist cities. Therefore, the results of this analysis of European competitors will be expounded upon.

It was an expensive project, since the research was conducted not only among tourists in Amsterdam, but also in some cities abroad, in order to assemble a representative picture of the European city tourist. These in-depth interviews were held in Amsterdam, Rome and Vienna. The research took place in four phases: first, deciding which European cities were the strongest competitors for Amsterdam, followed by analysis of the tourist's expectations of the city, analysis of what the city had to offer and analysis of the marketing efforts of the various cities.

The first component of the research provides a few surprises. Of the 34 cities that were rated, Barcelona, Copenhagen and Venice did not appear to be direct competitors for Amsterdam. On the other hand, Dublin, Edinburgh, Milan and Berlin were seen as competing directly for the tourist's favour.

The selection criteria were not so much the scope of tourist activity, as the degree to which the cities targeted the same markets as Amsterdam. Ultimately, ten cities were selected which provided genuine competition for Amsterdam. These were sub-jected to an extensive analysis.

ANALYSING THE DEMAND

The second step was to ask two questions: What does the tourist want from a city destination? How completely does Amsterdam fulfil these wishes? These questions can only be answered by gain-ing insight into the tourist's selection process. To this end, a survey was made of tourists in Amsterdam, Rome and Vienna, that pro-duced most interesting results. Once again, not only interesting for Amsterdam but for all those involved with tourist city marketing. The essential questions for us are: How does a tourist select a par-ticular city? How is a city evaluated according to these criteria?

Research showed that emotional criteria come first to the fore in a tourist's decision making. If a city has a weak or negative image, then it is immediately scrapped from the list. The tourist wants to feel relaxed in a city and welcome. Other emotional considerations influencing the tourist are atmosphere, friendli-ness of the people and street life.

Only after the consumer has conjured up a positive emotion from a name or picture of a city, do they move on to rational cri-teria. For instance: a city must have sufficient tourist attractions to justify a visit, and enough sights and activities to ensure full and satisfying days during the tourist's visit. The result of this interaction between emotional and rational criteria is responsi-ble for determining if a city appears at all on the tourist's long list. Only when the tourist is ready to narrow his choices further do practical aspects come into play, including the distance to be travelled, comfort, price, climate, etc.

The study also revealed which criteria are the most important for the consumer in choosing a city. The top three are atmosphere, history and museums. These are followed by tourist attractions and cultural offerings. Further down on the list lie aspects such as price level, safety, restaurants and public transport.

Obviously, a city's image is the overriding factor in the deci-sion making process. The potential visitor mostly knows about a city from family and friends, information through the mass media such as newspapers and television and promotional mate-rials (advertisements, brochures and posters). Based on this rather random assembling of information, the tourist creates a picture of the tourist destination and makes a final decision.

The competitor analysis shows that a tourist's perception of a city before and after a visit can change radically. In no other city under examination is that before-and-after phenomenon so strong as in Amsterdam. The most important criteria for making a choice – atmosphere, history and museums – get much higher marks after a visit than before. Amsterdam's image as a museum city for instance, seems to be extremely weak. Prior to a visit, Amsterdam scores a measly 5.5 on a scale of 1 to 10. Vienna earns a 9, Berlin a 7.5 and Munich a 6. After the visit, Vienna's rating goes down slightly to 8.8. But Amsterdam grows considerably in the public's estimation, leaping to an 8 plus.

Amsterdam has then a fairly obvious image problem. Although that can be seen as a kind of luxury problem (problems only really arise when a rating goes down after a visit), it is still an issue which must be addressed.

ANALYSING WHAT CITY HAS TO OFFER

Now that we are familiar with the decision making criteria, it has become simpler to evaluate the degree in which a city can satisfy the needs of the consumer as a potential client.

The things a city has to offer to the tourist can be represented graphically in a pyramid. In this model, a city's range of attractions is comprised of several determining elements. Unique sights which are a 'must' for the tourist, and which are critical to attract the first-time tourist to the city. Additionally, the city offers attractions which appeal to those staying for a longer period of time. This category is also important in stimulating repeat visits. The base consists of all other product elements which do not generate extra tourist visits, but which are nevertheless important to provide the tourist with a pleasant stay.

EXAMINING MARKETING EFFORTS

So we know what the city tourist is looking for and how, and to what degree, Amsterdam can offer what they want. The next step is to analyse the marketing efforts at work in Amsterdam and the other cities. How effective are these efforts in terms of supply and demand? What can be learned from them?

To summarise the most important findings.

- Shift the focus of activities from trade to consumer.

- Base promotional activities on consumer demand and not on the producer's supply.

- Shape promotional efforts to the various stages of the tourist's decision making process (from emotional phase to rational phase to practical phase to consumption to post-consumption).

In short, consumer demand must determine promotional activity, but this practice is not yet always commonplace in the tourist industry.

An important part of market approach is providing the tourist with information. Which means of communication are the most effective in influencing the city tourist? The on-the-street surveys conducted by the Amsterdam Tourist Office over the past year provide the answer to that question.

It is actually friends and family who are the tourist's single most important source of information. They are far more important than travel agencies or promotional brochures from the Amsterdam Tourist Office. They account for 76 per cent of the responses, followed by television programmes (71 per cent) and articles in newspapers and magazines.

When asked which source of information was the most important in making the decision to come to Amsterdam, hearsay appeared to be many times more influential than any other source. So, perhaps the best investment in promotion is an investment in the happy memories tourists take home.

A PRACTICAL LESSON

Well, we have all this information now, but what can we learn from it? What can we do with it? In two words: *make choices*.

- Choose consumer-oriented marketing activities.

- Choose a limited number of markets.

- Choose promotion of 'musts', instead of promoting the entire product.

- Choose co-operation pooling of resources with other organisations.

The larger more metropolitan cities possess most of Europe's culture both past and present. It is these that are the so-called European 'musts' for a visitor.

Capital cities are, therefore, in most cases visited first (by first users) and can be considered as 'teasers' for a country. Long-haul visitors tend to reside in larger metropolitan areas and move around the country from there. The importance of the capital cities to national tourism is thus much larger than is recognised normally, in particular by national governments and national tourist bodies.

The market for city trips has been stable during recent years. Although we suffered Chernobyl, the Gulf War, and economic recession, between 1986 and 1995 city tourism in 61 FECTO cities increased by 10 per cent. City tourism is very sustainable, which makes it interesting for investors, such as in real estate (hotels, attractions).

The main countries generating overnight visitors are: the UK, the USA, Germany, France, Italy and Spain. However, the largest growth worldwide is non-European: in 1986-1995 there was a 5 per cent increase from European countries, but 23 per cent from outside Europe.

European cities are not getting their fair share out of these markets. More growth from southeast Asia is expected, but the increase is not sufficient in Europe. On the other hand, the US market is a mature one: back to the roots effects will decrease in coming decades. Therefore a new European marketing approach is needed. A more consumer-oriented approach.

However, on the continent we have a tendency to think along nationalistic lines. We sincerely believe that the right approach is to promote our countries and only afterwards to promote the cities as part of that country. Because we know where and what our country is, we expect the customer to do so as well. Holland's approach until recently was that Holland should be promoted first, and then its capital, although the capital's name was more well known than that of the country. US citizens do not necessarily know where Amsterdam is, but they do know that it is somewhere in northern Europe: it may be the capital of Denmark? It does not matter whether they know specifically, as long as they go there.

Fifty-one per cent of French people do know Amsterdam by name, but have not the slightest idea what the distance is from Paris. But in the tourism business, we still prefer to teach geography first, instead of concentrating on the essentials for our business. We are very product oriented, when we should be making more effort to be customer oriented. This year Amsterdam is positioning itself in the USA in conjunction with London and Paris.

The cultural cities in Europe created a joint profile through Art Cities in Europe (ACE) in 1993. Based on the same simple starting point: the long haul customer only recognises 'Europe'. Therefore its number one product is the (capital) cities. We then should market everything together as 'Europe'. The European Union's DG 23 will support this in the near future. Marketing initiatives can be supported financially, whereas this was not possible before.

Most European joint marketing efforts until now were within country borders: such as the magic ten in Germany.

This is influenced by product-oriented behaviour: cities in the same country (you can trace the joint marketing concept if it is there, in cities within countries such as Florence, Rome and Siena in Italy or in Germany, Cologne, Bonn and Dusseldorf in Germany).

New approaches, such as city zapping, started only recently from the tour-operator side. Tourist offices are now offering Paris and London in one tour. Another tourist office is offering Prague, Vienna and Budapest.

Did you know that a third of all visitors to Amsterdam (national and foreign) combined the city with another one on the same tour?

Fifty-four per cent of all North American visitors entered Amsterdam, coming from another (European) destination. And what do the national tourist organisations do? Not very much until now.

If this self-oriented thinking is not addressed, Europe will miss market segments. It is time to think European, but even more important, to act European. Among the numerous European associations of tourist organisations and their directors, the common talk, it seems, is about our own problems and the similarity with each other's problems. But not much is done in terms of thinking of new directions and solutions.

In its early years, the Federation of European Tourist Offices (FECTO) had the same approach. However, since 1992 it went into a new direction: barriers were removed, understanding started and action was taken. We are now working on a pan-European information and reservation system on the Internet and are taking a similar approach to tourism information and the quality thereof.

We are now working on a way to set up common surveys in order to be able to compare figures, and we have started to exchange experiences and information and statistics. We have started a marketing concept for cultural cities called 'Art Cities' in Europe. With an uncommon, business-like approach acting as entrepreneurs, not waiting for more subsidies to come before we act. Maybe there are other initiatives of which I am not aware, in the same direction: to market Europe as one destination. I hope so, because this is the only way we will be able to keep our market share in world tourism.

Think European, act European, and don't bother if the grass in your neighbour's garden appears to be greener: if it is, you will benefit as well. We, in Amsterdam, found out in 1993, after the IPMG survey, that Dublin was doing extremely well. When I asked my FECTO colleague, Frank Magee, about his success he invited me right away to come to Dublin and told me all – and we learned a lot. And I suppose even he did. If one city in Europe pleases the customer, he is willing to try another. If his first visit was unsatisfactory, he may stay away from Europe.

The typical problems of metropolitan cities (i.e. criminality, accessibility, etc.) could also be better dealt with in a European way. City centres must remain open and closed: open in order to let the customer enter, closed in order to preserve historic city centres. Also there we could learn from each other. What lesson have we learned for instance from the coach ban in Salzburg? Do we share that experience? I am convinced we should and I hope you will be also.

We need each other. Let that be the real European experience.

TRENDS IN THE GROWTH OF URBAN TOURISM

Sheila Flanagan
Faculty of Tourism and Food, DIT

INTRODUCTION

This chapter examines current trends, developments and issues in relation to the growth of urban destinations from a tourism perspective. It will consider the international situation in the context of changing market demand, the development of urban and city tourism, the retailing and planning implications and current market segmentation.

Ireland is examined in the context of the growth of Dublin as a tourist destination, with city tourists being divided into two classes: short-stay holidaymakers and shoppers. The direct and indirect impact of city tourism is considered and the chapter concludes by reviewing the implications of the growth trends for Dublin as a tourism destination.

CHANGING MARKET DEMAND: THE INTERNATIONAL PERSPECTIVE

Some of the most pressing issues to confront the retailing, tourism and leisure industries in recent years are those which concern the combination and interface of retail and leisure (ETB, 1989). More and more tourism and leisure attractions are seeking retail opportunities which will increase revenue and customer satisfaction. Retailing at attractions is changing from being peripheral to being a key source of revenue. Such developments generate and pose research questions as to the establishment of links between the retail and tourism industries.

Over the past 25 years there has been a significant reduction in standard working hours, an increase in holiday entitlement and an increase in household disposable income resulting in increased spending power and leisure time. In the Republic of Ireland, living standards have been converging on European levels over the past two decades. Per capita GNP rose from under 60 per cent of the EU average in 1970 to over 80 per cent in 1995. Common holiday entitlement has doubled so that today 99 per cent of full-time manual employees are entitled to four or more week's holiday per year. Closely allied to income and time is mobility.

The number of cars per thousand of the UK population rose by 44 per cent between 1971 and 1987 (Annual Bulletin of Transport Statistics). By 2001, in the UK there will be 1.2 million more children under 15, but there will be 4 million more people over 65, indicating the greying of that society. In the Republic of Ireland, population structure is less characterised by an aging society. The population of the State in 1996 was estimated to be 3.62 million. Approximately 46 per cent of the population is under 25 and the proportion of working age (15-64) is 64 per cent. Society is becoming more middle class as changes in job status favour those in the service sector. The family unit is becoming smaller and it is projected that one in three people will live alone in 2001 (ETB, 1989). The outcome of increased mobility, changing household structure and higher standards of living is that people are willing and able to travel significant distances for shopping and leisure purposes thus widening the catchment areas of these facilities. This has important implications for both the tourism and retail industries.

Tourism is now the largest industry and generator of jobs worldwide, accounting for more than 200 million jobs and representing 6 per cent of the EU's GDP (Papoutsis, 1995). The international tourism market has grown substantially over the past twenty years to the extent that market segments and geographic markets have established their own separate identities with different characteristics. The number of mini mass markets has grown each with very different changing characteristics.

One important, changing trend affecting Europe in general is the slow but continuing decline in the average length of trips and the amount of time spent at destinations. This still varies considerably from country to country from, for example, 11.4 days average for foreign visits in the UK to 3.7 days in Switzerland. This change is related to greater frequency of travel and more journeys, and it is a trend that is likely to continue. Seasonal flows have undergone some profound changes – so much so that seasonality is now regarded internationally as a challenge rather than a problem. Many of the old constraints, such as school terms, conditions of work and family ties, have fallen away but there are still traditional forces and inertia which resist change. Therein lies the marketing challenge which is to even out the seasonal peaks and troughs.

The creation of specialist travel flows (shopping, conferences, crafts, weekend short breaks and festivals) demonstrates once again the increasing segmentation in the market, the importance of mini-market flows and the vast potential demand still to be realised.

URBAN AND CITY TOURISM

City tourism is a major growth sector which is out of peak oriented (Quest, 1990). Although many capital cities, metropolitan centres and historic towns and cities are important tourist destinations, urban areas have been relatively neglected by tourism researchers. The work that has been done has been primarily morphological, focusing on the distribution of different forms of accommodation. Other writers have examined aspects of planning, demand and the economic impact of tourism. While these morphological studies have taken account of changing patterns of accommodation over time, little explicit attention has been paid to processes of tourist development in urban areas.

Towns and cities, perhaps more than any other areas, are multi-functional in nature. This factor conditions the form tourism takes and the way in which it develops. Tourists visit urban areas for a variety of reasons, such as entertainment and nightlife, to appreciate historical and cultural attractions, to attend major sporting or festival events, to shop or just to enjoy the charm and character of a particular city. Many cities also receive a considerable volume of traffic generated by other contemporary functions (Getz, 1993). Administration, commerce and industry attract large numbers of business travellers while a sizeable resident population will generate a significant number of visits from friends and relatives. Conferences and special events will draw other visitors. These functions and attractions vary from city to city, with many North American cities perhaps being less dependent than European ones on historical and cultural attractions while drawing more of their visitors for business, conventions, entertainment and from visits to purpose-built attractions, such as theme parks.

CITY TOURISM:
RETAILING AND PLANNING IMPLICATIONS

Tourism retailing has been described as big business and is forecast to become even bigger. Little attention has been paid to the role of shopping as an attraction and research has focused on shopping within hotels, attractions, events and new tourism concepts. In general, tourism and retailing are not associated, but any analysis on the behaviour of tourists will show that a significant amount of time and money is spent on shopping (Law, 1993). The British Tourist Authority, for example, has estimated that the average tourist to Britain spends approximately 27 per cent of their total tourism budget on shopping alone.

Many of the published visitor surveys confirm that tourists spend a lot of time and money on shopping, but such studies shed little light on whether shopping is a trip motivator or how a destination's attributes might influence travel and shopping patterns (Getz, 1993). However, shopping is an integral part of the tourist's experience and comprises a major use of time for many visitors regardless of their primary travel motivations. Therefore, the spatial relationship of tourist activities must be related to hotel and transportation as a precondition of synergism. The creation of intervening shopping opportunities along predictable sightseeing routes is one of the most effective planning instruments in developing the tourism potential of an urban area.

As tourist demand is heavily dependent on other urban functions, so changes in these functions will influence the path of tourist development. As the central location of many city hotels reflects demand generated by other central functions, it follows that changes in the distribution of hotels will result from an expansion of the central business district (CBD) or the appearance of new centres as well as from a shortage of sites. The evolution of hotels in Madrid shows how there has been a progressive shift from the Puerta del Sol to the north and northeast as administrative and commercial activities have developed in that direction. A similar pattern occurs in Lisbon, where the Avenida da Libertade links the older, smaller hotels of the centre with the more recent, larger better hotels in the streets surrounding the Parque Eduardo VII, also an area of recent expansion.

Elsewhere, tourism is adopted as a rationale for the preservation of historic quarters or is identified as a key element in urban renewal projects. A range of US cities where the tourist element has been an integral part of the preservation of downtown cores or the adjacent zone of discard include Charlestown, the French Quarter of New Orleans and Pioneer Square in Seattle. Baltimore, San Francisco and Boston are all cities where tourism has been incorporated into urban revitalisation. However, the success of the tourist industry in each case will depend on the extent to which private investment is stimulated by such developments.

City tourism has not been limited to preservation projects. In Paris, for example, planning authorities have sought some diversity in their renewal or redevelopment projects by encouraging hotel construction amongst large office complexes through offering land for hotels at half the rate for office buildings. The Sheraton, for example, forms part of the Ilot Vandamme renewal project. Changes in the importance of modes of transport have also seen the appearance of hotels located along autoroutes on the outskirts of the city, particularly those belonging to the French Novotel chain and the growth of 3 and 4-star hotels around both Orly and Charles de Gaulle airports.

URBAN TOURISM MARKET SEGMENTATION

A number of specific markets have been identified at international level and are developing in the context of city tourism. The market can be segmented into the following key groupings.

1. Short-break destinations.

2. Shopping: general shopping, specialist retail shopping and cross border shopping.

3. Festivals and events.

1. Short-break Destinations

The short-break market is now the fastest growing sector of the European travel market (Quest, 1990). Germany is the major market generating about a third of all short-break trips in 1991 and France the main destination, with about a 20 per cent market share. Short-break holidays of between one and three nights are the fastest growing sector of the UK holiday market, growing at a rate of 20 per cent between 1990 and 1993. Approximately 10 per cent of the population of the UK take them, mainly in the Spring and Autumn and such groups tend to be upwardly mobile executives or over the age of 45. Demand from such groups springs from high disposable income and reduced family constraints. Factors, such as the development of the Channel Tunnel and new holiday products such as Center Parcs and EuroDisney, have opened up the short-break market in the UK. Over 920 million day trips are made each year in the UK alone. Families tend to visit specific attractions whilst older parties are more attracted to a place or area for their day trip excursion. This trend is expected to continue (ETB, 1989).

Cities are interested in the short-break market. Of major interest is the fact that the average spend per night is two and a half times higher than for trips of four nights or more. In addition there is a more even spread of travel throughout the year. Most city hotels offer special cut prices at weekends and many arrange tickets for entertainment at the same time. With the city-break market, Paris remains the most popular destination, followed by Amsterdam. There is increasing interest in more distant European cities such as Rome and Prague and short-breaks overseas appeal more to couples travelling without children.

The Economist (1995) predicts that many of Asia's future tourists will take several short breaks every year rather than one long holiday break. Cebu in the Philippines and Cairns in northeast Australia are becoming popular among tourists from Singapore and Hong Kong.

2. Shopping

General Patterns

Increasingly, people are spending their leisure time shopping and it is not surprising that they should wish to do so while on holiday. The English Tourist Board and Jones Lang Wooton published, in 1989/90, what is thought to be the first significant study of retail, leisure and tourism. This study highlights the point that shopping is a prime ingredient in total leisure spend and is an important part of the leisure experience in the UK and worldwide.

Sixty per cent of all overseas visitors to the UK pass through London, and while there, they spend an estimated £500 million a year in Oxford Street alone which accounts for 14 per cent of this street's total turnover. Department stores remain important in leisure shopping. In London, the main department store destinations include Harrods, Liberty, Selfridges and Marks & Spencer. In Paris, it's Galleries Lafayette; in Amsterdam it's De Bijenkorf and

in North America it's Bloomingdale's, Macy's, Henri Bendel and
Saks Fifth Avenue. Harrods is the first and often only shopping
stop of many London tourists. Tourism is key to Harrods, contributing an estimated 50 per cent of its turnover, which averages
£700,000 from 50,000 customers a day, no less than 40 per cent of
whom are from abroad. During the peak season, approximately 75
per cent of Harrods' customers are tourists, predominately from
North America, spending about £20 each on average.

According to Kent *et al* (1983) shopping ranked as the most
popular activity among all tourist-visitors surveyed in the
Atlanta and Georgia region, with expenditures on shopping
accounting for 18 per cent of the total. The researchers advocat-
ed more emphasis on shopping in tourism advertising. A similar
trend can be shown by examining the breakdown of overseas
and domestic tourist expenditure in the UK in 1991.

Table 4.1: Tourist Expenditure in the UK

Accommodation	34.9%
Eating and Drinking	24.1%
Travel within the UK	14%
Shopping	18.9%
Entertainment	5.5%
Other	2.6%

Source: Law, 1993

Law's estimates for shopping differ from those of BTA (27 per
cent) which highlights the intrinsic difficulties involved in com-
piling a single figure for tourist shopping. However, it is true to
say that in every case the tourism income multiplier effect (TIM)
has been found to be as high as £2.50 for every pound of tourist
spending. The English Tourist Board has carried out a number of
visitor expenditure surveys in Winchester and Bournemouth. In
Bournemouth, 71 per cent of holidaymakers and 53 per cent of
day trippers undertook or planned to shop during their stay.
Shopping was the highest on the list of activities, ahead of visiting places of interest, swimming or eating out. In Winchester
more than £4 out of every £5 was spent in shops, restaurants,
cafes, pubs and attractions in the city. Interestingly, day visitors
spent more on shopping than staying visitors.

Many developers are now making a concerted effort to appeal
to the tourist market in the US. Mega-multi malls are being

developed to cater for tourists as well as the local population. Two such examples are the West Edmonton Mall, Alberta, Canada and the Mall of America in Minnesota. Both combine a very large shopping centre with a theme park and it is estimated that the West Edmonton Mall attracts 5 million tourists per annum accounting for £227 million in revenue.

Speciality Retailing

Tourists are particularly attracted by what is now termed 'speciality' retailing. Among the goods sold under this heading we can include crafts, pottery, designer clothing, books and unusual household articles. Tourists are particularly attracted to these products and services which they perceive as being unique or unusual and which add to the tourist experience. In the UK, the Brindleyplace development next to Birmingham International Conference Centre and the Deansgate Centre retail and leisure complex, beside the Greater Manchester Exhibition Centre are examples of locations where the speciality retailing concept has been developed. Similar to Covent Garden in London, these are designed to attract tourists to an environment which is totally different from the traditional high street, which is often dominated by the multiples.

Developers are becoming more aware of the advantages of including leisure activities within or close to retailing functions. The UK out of town centres, such as the MetroCentre in Gateshead and Merry Hill in Dudley, are planning hotels and a wide range of leisure facilities, such as Metroland, an indoor theme park. In the past fifteen years, new hybrids have appeared on the UK retail scene – speciality centres, mixed-use centres and retail parks. Speciality centres can be of any size and are marketed on a continual basis as a themed development. These would include festival marketplaces, fashion centres and home centres. RHS Enterprises in Wisley Garden is an example of such a development. Access from the M25 has ensured attendance figures in excess of 750,000 per annum. The shop and plant centre are located at the entrance and can be used without entering the gardens themselves, thus encouraging people to make repeat visits to simply go shopping, if they so wish.

Mixed-use centres include retail, hotel, office, leisure, cultural and convention facilities. The MetroCentre in Gateshead is the largest retail leisure development in the UK, with almost 2 million square feet of undercover leisure and shopping. There are

297 retailers (including 6 department stores), a food court, multi-screen cinema and leisure area called MetroLand. Parking is available for 5,000 vehicles.

Retail parks are clusters of larger scale, superstore or ware-house retailers typically located on the outside of town and are favoured by many developers and shoppers. All provide opportunities for combing retail and leisure. The Clarks Retail Outlet in Street, Somerset is one such example.

Cross Border Shopping

Cross border shopping is a retail tourism phenomenon which is often overlooked and is an aspect of tourism that fluctuates greatly with macro-economic conditions. Cross border shopping can be observed at border points such as those between the Republic of Ireland and Northern Ireland, Italy and Switzerland, Canada and the US and west Poland and Germany.

3. Festivals and Events

Davidson (1995) reports that festival events in the US are among the fastest growing segments of tourism. Countries and cities compete vigorously for mega events such as the Olympic Games, World Cup and World Fairs. In Europe there is a renewed growth in arts and festivals. *The Economist* (1995) reports a revival in the cultural life of Naples after years of decay. The city's Napolic Porte Aperte project, which was an attempt to create an open museum to feature monuments and churches within selected neighbourhoods, attracted so many visitors that it was hard to find a hotel room. Genoa's new opera director is lengthening the season and anticipating it with more adventurous imports and joint productions from international festivals.

An astonishing manifestation of the arts has taken root in Edinburgh. Edinburgh's international festival which started in August 1947 has not only survived but it has attracted to Edinburgh a huge diversity of other events such as film festivals, book festivals, television and jazz festivals.

URBAN TOURISM IN IRELAND

The National Perspective

The EU operational programme for tourism – Tourism 2000 – outlines the contribution which tourism makes to the national economy. It is estimated that tourism in Ireland, including home holidays, is now a £2 billion a year industry.

In 1997, almost 119,300 people were fully employed in tourism and related sectors, an increase of almost 52,000 since 1988. In fact, tourism-related jobs accounted for roughly half of the net increase in national employment from 1988-1993 and it accounts for almost 8.8 per cent of all employment in the economy.

Tourism is also perceived as a driving force of national economic expansion, particularly through its foreign exchange earnings. Since most inputs in the tourism industry are home-produced, tourism earnings have a high multiplier effect in terms of national income. The direct import content of tourism is as low as 10 per cent, which implies that 90 per cent of foreign earnings are retained within the national economy. In fact, tourism's share of GNP went from 5.8 per cent to 6.3 per cent between 1988 and 1997.

Tourism is also viewed by government as being a powerful instrument in assisting the raising of incomes and providing employment in the country's more remote and poorer regions. It is also pointed out in the operational programme that tourism has the important added value effect of energising and raising the morale of communities in regions which have been adversely affected by emigration and depopulation.

A Dublin Regional Perspective

The number of out of State visitors staying in the Dublin region for one night or more has grown by from 1,693,000 in 1993 to 2,696,000 in 1997. 2.4 million bednights were booked in the Dublin Tourism Information and Reservations centres in 1997 (see Table 4.2).

In terms of revenue, Britain is currently the biggest source of revenue in the Dublin context, but continental Europe has increased in importance. The continental European market yielded £166.1 million in revenue in 1997 while North America accounted for £94.3 million. Britain yielded 179.9 million in tourism revenue in 1997.

Table 4.2: Number of Tourist Visits to the Dublin Region (000s)

	1993	1997
Britain	657	1,313
Continental Europe	500	652
North America	268	480
Other areas	84	141
Total overseas tourists	1,509	2,586
Domestic tourism	1,266	989
Northern Ireland	184	110
Total tourists	2,959	3,685

Perspectives on Existing Tourist Profile

Approximately 49 per cent of all tourist visits to the Dublin region take place between June and September with a higher proportion (61 per cent) of holidaymaker trips occurring in this period. The strong business market and the Scandinavian shopping trips contribute to a more even seasonal distribution.

In 1997, overseas holidaymakers stayed in Dublin for 4.9 nights, on average. The average duration of stay compares well with that recorded for a number of other urban destinations, including Singapore (3.6 days) and Amsterdam (2.2 days) The average length of stay of all overseas visitors to Edinburgh is 5.8 days.

Tourists visiting Dublin tend to see the sights, visit historic places, museums and art galleries, go to theatres, shows, music venues and pubs, go shopping and eat out. Many engage in active pursuits during their holiday in Ireland including walking, cycling, golf and fishing but the extent to which they engage in these while in the Dublin region is uncertain according to the 1994 CHL "Tourism to Dublin – Marketing for Growth" report. Opportunities exist for tourists who use Dublin as a base to engage in the range of the above passive and active pursuits.

This can be achieved through:

- the development of festivals;

- co-ordination of historical assets;

- development of integrated activity packages;

- creation of a golf co-operative;

- the development of a more effective tourism information network using access points including Dublin Port and Dublin Airport.

Approximately 41 per cent of all tourists to Ireland are holiday-makers and 21 per cent visit for business reasons. In 1997, 86,000 international conference delegates came to Ireland with 72 per cent spending at least one night in the capital. In addition 18,000 incentive travellers came to Ireland in 1997 with 65 per cent spending at least one night in Dublin. The Dublin region is unique in that there is a distinct split between business and holiday tourists.

The Dublin Tourism Draft Regional Development Plan, 1993-1997 states that since 1988 the total investment in new tourism products and facilities in Dublin now stands in excess of £235 million. This is the biggest ever investment in tourism in the region. With necessary investment and support from the public and private sectors, the potential for further job creation can be realised through the growth and expansion of tourism in Dublin. It is accepted that each £1 million of foreign revenue in Dublin will generate an additional 52 new jobs and each £1 million of domestic revenue will generate an additional 40 new jobs.

The objective of Dublin Tourism's Draft Development Plan is to generate new jobs in Dublin city and county by increasing foreign revenue. This will be achieved by:

- increasing the numbers of visitors to Dublin;

- extending the length of stay;

- attracting higher spending visitors;

- capitalising on Dublin's role as Ireland's capital city;

- marketing the capital to provincial Ireland to increase home holiday numbers.

Urban Tourism: The Dublin Perspective

Dublin has begun to realise its potential as a major European city destination. According to ITIC (1996) a significant part of this increase in tourism to the city is 'destination specific' and the growth to Dublin should not be viewed as displacement tourism (in other words occurring at the expense of other regions). The dramatic growth in Dublin and its hinterland is due to increased demand for city tourism and the growing number of visitors using Dublin as a gateway. The marked increase in share of Ireland's tourists visiting and staying in the city reflects an increase in two categories of holiday visitors: city tourists and gateway tourists. In the case of city tourists, the sole or principal motivation is to visit Dublin which is currently Ireland's only urban destination which can effectively compete with other high profile UK and European cities.

Among tourism analysts, Dublin is now recognised as one of the most popular cities in Europe for short-term visitors and weekend breaks. Despite appearances, the city is not just attractive to English stag party organisers. The developing 'street tourism' in such areas as Temple Bar has been a critical factor in enhancing the capital's appeal. A wider range of tourist attractions and their greater accessibility by virtue of longer opening hours has made Dublin "an eighteen hour per day tourist city" according to Tom Coffey of the Dublin City Centre Business Association.

Hotels, retailers and carriers all reported tourism figures to be up by at least 15 per cent for the period January to August 1995. Dublin Chamber of Commerce research showed the following.

- Top hotels in the city are showing an upswing in business between 10-20 per cent on 1994. The biggest increases are among tourist visitors from the UK and the US, while domestic and European markets are also performing well.

- Retailers in the city and in suburban shopping centres are also benefiting from higher tourism numbers, with sales of tourism-related goods up by as much as 15 per cent in many stores.

- Passenger carriers into Dublin are bringing more people into the country than at any other time. Airlines are reporting increases in passenger numbers of up to 26 per cent per cent for the continental market between 1993 and 1997, with good growth also in the US and UK market.

- Air passenger traffic through Dublin airport rose from 5 million in 1991 to 11 million in 1997. Stena Sealink carried 1.4 million passengers in 1994 through Dun Laoghaire port representing a rise of 17 per cent on 1993. The company reports strong demand from short-stay tourists from the UK in recent months and expects a greater demand given the high speed service (HSS) is now in full operation. Both Stena Sealink and Irish Ferries increased capacity by 139 per cent and 137 per cent respectively between 1991-1996.

The Irish Hotels Federation cites the increased number of flights into Dublin and promotional efforts by the industry as reasons for the success of Dublin and its hinterland. People visiting Dublin are far more likely to be short-staying visitors. In 1993, only two in five visitors to Dublin said that holidaymaking was the main purpose of their visit. However, Dublin is well placed to take advantage of this international trend towards urban tourism and short city breaks. Alternatives, such as international conferences, sporting events, festivals and other activities, need further development, particularly to increase visitor numbers during the low season.

City or urban tourists to Dublin can be divided into two classes:

1. short-stay holidaymakers;

2. shoppers.

1. Short-Break Holidays

According to the Irish Tourism Industry Confederation (1996), the trend, since 1989, has been towards short-stay holidays. Holidays of one to five night duration have increased in market share from 18 per cent in 1989 to 22 per cent in 1995. The most significant shift has been amongst British holidaymakers with 28 per cent now staying for less than six days. A similar trend can be found with European visitors. Market changes in short-break travel in the early-1990s have resulted in a steady increase in the city breaks, which accounted for close to one third of all trips.

The poularity of city breaks or urban tourism in general, has most certainly been boosted by the growth in the number and range of package programmes on offer since the beginning of the 1990s. Two important factors affecting urban tourism are access and accommodation. Since 1993, Ireland has enjoyed a significant increase in available scheduled air capacity to and from Britain and mainland Europe. Over the past two years, scheduled capacity on routes between Dublin and Britain has grown by 45 per cent, to an estimated 6.6 million seats. Capacity on scheduled continental European routes grew by 26 per cent over the period. Due to the introduction of larger ships, high speed ferries and increased frequencies on sea routes between Ireland and Britain, there has been an increase in capacity on services offered by Stena Sealink and Irish Ferries. The number of visitors arriving by sea has grown by 25 per cent to 1.14 million since 1993.

In terms of visitor accommodation, national room capacity increased by 40 per cent between 1989 and 1994. The total number of approved rooms (hotels, town and country, self-catering and hostel) increased by 49 per cent from 7,475 in 1990 to 11,137 in 1994 and the trend continues (see Table 4.3).

Table 4.3: Approved Accommodation Dublin

Year	1990	1991	1992	1993	1994	1995	1996
Rooms	7,475	8,220	8,767	9,308	11,137	13,000	13,721

Source: Dublin Tourism

Hotels in Dublin achieved a significantly higher utilisation over the period 1989 to 1995 recording a 15 per cent increase in average room occupancy to a peak of 79 per cent which is well above the national average occupancy of 67 per cent.

2. Shoppers

Shopping has been highlighted as a product for development in Irish tourism by the operational programme 1989-1993. Bord Fáilte wish to push out the boundaries of tourism as a force for economic regeneration by focusing on a segment of the market that can be attracted specifically for the quality of Ireland's shopping. Tourists so attracted are not just very high spenders but their expenditure is concentrated on the best of Irish traditional goods. Such speciality shopping tours are more easily stimulated outside the peak summer season which, in turn, helps improve the spread of business through out the year. Bord Fáilte have been critical of the retail trade for their lack of support in relation to the marketing of the Irish scene in general and they point to the fact that, for many outlets, the quest for tourism has not risen above the questionable practice of paying commission to coach drivers and tour guides to lure their charges into particular shops.

Dublin Tourism marketing staff attend workshops in key market areas where significant growth in urban is expected including London, Benelux and Iceland. The Dublin City marketing initiative continues to attract visitors from Northern Ireland and Britain in increasing numbers. One of the main developments in recent years has been the growth in visitor numbers from Iceland. This pre-Christmas initiative attracted over 7,000 visiting Icelandic shoppers to the city in 1997. This augmented the revenue of city stores at a time when other visitors to the city are relatively low. The initiative is worth £9.2 million to the city – an average spend of £1,314 per visitor. While the Icelanders are high users of hotel and restaurants, shopping is an important motivation in view of the high VAT and excise duties which operate in their home country. Samvinn Travel, who have made Dublin their primary destination for Icelanders taking short-break holidays, have jointly, with Dublin Tourism, produced a special shopping guide to Dublin and in 1998 the company are offering alternative city short breaks to Cork and a fly-drive package to Galway. The lucrative Iceland-Dublin city break business is also sought after by several competing English and Scottish destinations including Bristol, Newcastle and Edinburgh.

Bord Fáilte also identifies the importance of this shopping market and this is demonstrated by the fact that Samvinn Travel, Iceland's largest tour operator (32 per cent market share) have made Dublin their primary destination for short-break holidays. The foremost strength of the Irish tourism product as perceived by Samvinn is the positive attitude of the Irish to tourism along with the flexibility and willingness to solve problems as they arise. Ireland is regarded as a place of excellent value both for shopping and good fun, hence Samvinn Travel has invested more money and effort than any other destination. They use full colour page advertisements in newspapers and television commercials to promote Ireland and thus in association with Bord Fáilte and Dublin Tourism, they strongly believe that Dublin and Ireland is a future destination, not only for Icelanders but for Europeans in general.

Linked to shopping tourism are other activities including conference promotion. A total of 228 international conferences were held in Dublin in 1994, with a total of 69,020 delegates attending. This generated £69 million in foreign revenue earnings

(Convention Bureau of Ireland, 1995). Within 1998, Ireland will have hosted 103,000 conference and incentive delegates generating £100 million in tourism revenue. The conference sector of the tourism industry is considered to be the most valuable to the economy as conference delegates are among the highest spending visitors. Conference business from Britain alone generated 44,000 visitors and revenue estimated at IR£22 million in Ireland in 1998.

Dublin tourism together with Dublin corporation and the administrative councils have engaged in a number of promotional activities to develop Dublin as an urban tourism destination. In 1995 Dublin Tourism opened a tourist information office in the Square Shopping Centre in Tallaght in recognition of the potential which the centre offers from a tourism perspective. A similar venture is planned with the developers of the Blanchardstown Town Centre – Green properties. A jointly produced promotional video on Dublin helped to secure the Cutty Sark Tall Ships race for August 1998. Dublin Chamber of Commerce report that more than 930,000 visitors were in Dublin over four days to witness the final stages of the race and it is estimated that betwwenn 5-10 per cent of these were non-Irish nationals. Other major sporting events that attract large visitor numbers are the Five Nations Rugby tournament and the American Football collegiate games, both of which are held in the off-season.

Indirect Commercial Impacts of Shopping Tourism

Dublin Chamber of Commerce figures for 1995 show that over 9 per cent of business revenue in Dublin is generated by tourism. This amount to almost £905 million. Almost half of the businesses surveyed by the Chamber of Commerce stated that they earn some part of their turnover from tourism. While the percentage of turnover generated by tourism is greatest in sectors such as hotels, restaurants and related suppliers, the manufacturing and financial sectors also benefit. Average earnings generated by tourism are as follows.

Manufacturing	6%
Retail and distribution	5%
Financial services	2%
Other (general services)	16%

The figure for retail and distribution does not reflect the 10-12 per cent of income generated by tourism in the larger city centre outlets and this figure is higher again for some speciality shops and goods.

The figures show the importance of tourism to jobs in Dublin, where 31,600 full-time job equivalents are supported by the sector. The tourist pound benefits more than just those directly involved in the industry. It affects builders, supermarkets, financial institutions, retailers, transport providers and many others.

Implications of Tourism growth trends for Dublin as a Destination

This review of tourism to Dublin has drawn a positive picture of Dublin's tourism performance over the past 65 years. The main findings are that:

- tourism is a growth business for Dublin, generating substantial employment and incomes in many sectors, including retailing;

- Dublin has generally outperformed the national growth rate and the growth rates recorded by a number of other competing destinations;

- tourism in Dublin makes a valuable contribution to national economic targets in terms of employment, GNP and tax revenues.

The current challenge is to ensure that the achievements in the growth and development of Dublin's tourism industry over the past six years are consolidated and built upon up to the year 2000. Investment in creative and effective marketing will have a crucial role to play in keeping Dublin on a growth path in a highly competitive marketplace.

REFERENCES

Bord Fáilte, (1994) *Developing Sustainable Tourism* (Dublin).

Davidson, Thomas Lea (1995) "What are Travel and Tourism: Are they really an Industry? in William F Theobald (ed.), *Global Tourism - The Next Decade* (Butterworth Heinemann, Oxford).

Dublin Tourism (1997) *Annual Report* (Dublin).

Dublin Tourism (1997) *Tourism Facts for the Dublin Region*, (Dublin).

English Tourist Board & Jones Lang Wooton (1989) *Retail, Leisure and Tourism* (London).

Getz, Donald (1993) *"Tourist Shopping Villages, Development and Management Strategies Tourism Management"* Vol. 14, No. 1. pp. 15-26.

Go, Frank M and Pine, Ray (1995) *Globalisation Strategy in the Hotel Industry* (Routledge, New York).

Jansen-Verbeke, M (1990) "Leisure and Shopping Tourism Product Mix" in G Ashworth & B Goodall (eds) *Marketing Tourism* J18.

Mills, Stephen (1990) "The Development of New Tourism Products" in Quest, Miles (ed.) *Horwarth Book of Tourism* (Macmillan Press Ltd, London).

Papoutsis, Christos (1995) "Why Tourist Numbers don't tell the Whole Story" *The European* May 1996.

Pearce, D (1987) *Tourism Today: A Geographical Analysis* (Longman, London).

AIRPORTS: FACILITATING ECONOMIC GROWTH

Oliver Costello

Head of Commercial Activities and Deputy General Manager, Aer Rianta

INTRODUCTION

In discussing the role of airports in facilitating regional economic growth, it is the intention of this chapter to focus on the practical perspective of Aer Rianta, with particular reference to Dublin Airport. This chapter examines the following issues.

- The role of airports.

- What is Dublin Airport?

- How does Dublin Airport facilitate economic growth?

- Infrastructural plans.

- Funding the development programme.

- The role of duty free.

THE ROLE OF AIRPORTS

At first glance, the role of an airport may appear fairly obvious, i.e. to act as a 'bridge' for people entering and leaving a particular location. This indeed is correct, but today's airports tend to be more complex. It is useful to view airports generically according to a number of scales.

Utility	<....................>	Enterprise
Dependent	<....................>	Independent
Passive	<....................>	Proactive
Franchiser	<....................>	Operator

In general, the more an airport acts as a utility franchiser and is dependent, the more dependent it is on forces outside its control, as a result, the airport behaves as a non-commercial public utility. By contrast, the more an airport acts as an independent-proactive entrepreneurial operator, the more it is capable of influencing its own destiny and behaving as an independent business entity. Aer Rianta sees itself as an enterprise with core airport businesses in the areas of airport ownership, airport management, duty free retailing and supply services. This enterprise approach has enabled Aer Rianta to not only develop its core and non-core businesses in Ireland, but also to expand in a significant way on the international front.

WHAT IS DUBLIN AIRPORT?

Dublin Airport is:

- an airport used by 9.1 million passengers in 1996 (11.6m in 1998);

- possibly the biggest, economic unit in Ireland;

- home to about 110 separate businesses;

- a major retail environment with 33 separate shops generating turnover of about £75 million in 1996;

- an economic zone which accounts for about 2.1 per cent of GNP;

- the place of employment of about 9,000 people directly, and the source of employment of about another 35,000 indirectly;

- an airport serving 60 scheduled passenger routes servicing:
  - 23 UK destinations;
  - 26 European destinations;
  - 5 transatlantic destinations;
  - 6 domestic destinations;

- served by 24 scheduled airlines;

- an airport used by 90 per cent of the top 1,000 Irish companies;

- one of the fastest-growing airports of its size.

Table 5.1 shows that passenger traffic at Dublin Airport has increased from 2.6 million in 1985 to 9.1 million in 1996, an increase of over 300 per cent. It is expected that the number of passengers will probably exceed 12,000,000 by the year 2000 (13 million prediction for 1999).

Table 5.1: Passenger Traffic at Dublin Airport

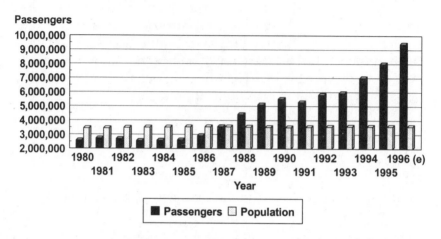

Passengers ■ Population

HOW DOES DUBLIN AIRPORT FACILITATE REGIONAL ECONOMIC GROWTH

Dublin airport facilitates regional economic growth through the following mechanisms.

- By keeping charges to airline customers as low as possible.

- By providing high quality facilities and services.

- By actively pursuing market development opportunities.

- By adopting a partnership approach to development with community and business interests.

Low-Cost Airport Charges

At the heart of Aer Rianta's strategy for facilitating low-cost access into Ireland lies a policy of having extremely competitive airport charges.

- Dublin Airport's charges have not increased at all since 1987.

- Substantial discounts and incentive schemes have been introduced over that time period.

The average charge per passenger at Dublin Airport was 32 per cent cheaper in 1995 than it was in 1988. This average was further reduced in 1996 and is expected to continue this pattern of decrease. A discount of 25 per cent has been applied to passenger load fees on routes to the UK and 50 per cent discount on scheduled landing charges from November to March. A 90 per cent discount for the first three years, and 70 per cent discount for the subsequent two years, on all *growth* on existing scheduled routes and all *new* scheduled routes.

Independent studies, not commissioned by the Department of Transport, Energy and Communications, have consistently shown Aer Rianta's charges at Dublin Airport to be among the lowest in Europe.

Another study of airport charges in Europe by Symonds, Travers and Morgan (in 1996) showed that Aer Rianta's charges at Dublin Airport were the 14th lowest out of the eighteen airports surveyed.

This extremely competitive regime of airport charges has been brought about by, among other things, a high level of cost consciousness and continuous productivity increases at Dublin Airport. For example, between 1991 and 1995, the number of passenger processed per man year of employment increased by almost 40 per cent.

High-quality Facilities and Services

Today's customers rightly demand the highest standard of facilities and services. In relation to services, the airport process is essentially a service business from the customers point of view, and the airport experience will be the first and last impression a visitor will have of a particular country.

Aer Rianta has defined a commitment to customer service and the quest for excellence as being among our core values. Some of the tangible ways in which these commitments manifest themselves at Dublin airport are as follows.

- Irish Quality Association Service Sector Quality Award (1992).

- First airport in the world to achieve ISO9002 certification (1993).

- First airport in the world to achieve accreditation to the International Environmental Standard ISO14001 (1996).

- Duty Free Retailer of the Year (1990).

- Best Value Perfumery in Europe (1994).

- Liquor Retailer of the Year (1995).
- "Dublinisation" programme.
- Christmas homecoming.

Through the creation of a high-quality service environment, Dublin Airport, contributes to the creation of a positive image of Ireland generally and of Dublin in particular.

Market Development

Dublin Airport can *influence* traffic development and not just respond passively to growth. Of course, a key mechanism of Aer Rianta's traffic development strategy at Dublin Airport has been the discount and incentive scheme designed to promote traffic growth. This scheme has been successful as indicated by passenger growth figures. What has been particularly striking has been the way in which the incentive scheme has promoted *competition on key routes*, and the beneficial effect of this competition. Through the examination of Manchester, Birmingham and Glasgow routes where competition has been introduced, evidence of growth is clear.

Table 5.2: Manchester

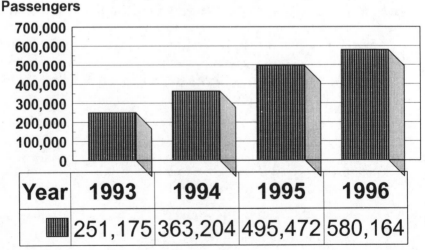

Manchester (+130%)
Served by more than one airline

Year	1993	1994	1995	1996
	251,175	363,204	495,472	580,164

Table 5.3: Birmingham

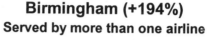

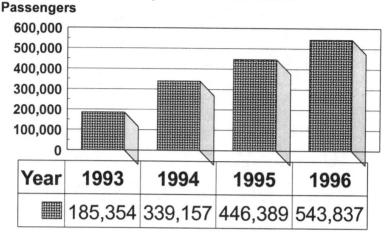

Year	1993	1994	1995	1996
	185,354	339,157	446,389	543,837

Table 5.4 Glasgow

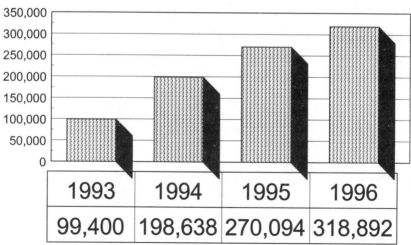

1993	1994	1995	1996
99,400	198,638	270,094	318,892

On the other hand, where there is no competition on a route, the story is entirely different, as you can see from the Barcelona case.

Table 5.5: Barcelona

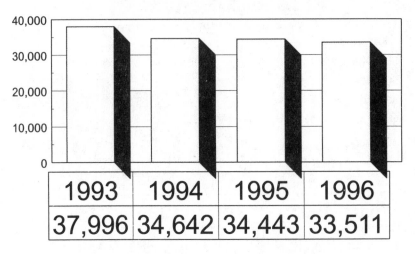

Impact of NO Competition: Barcelona

1993	1994	1995	1996
37,996	34,642	34,443	33,511

It is not solely in the area of competitive airport charges that Dublin Airport contributes to market development. In recent years, market research on the potential of a variety of routes into Dublin has been carried out. A very detailed route-profitability model has been developed to enable Aer Rianta to assess the likely viability of particular routes, and this model has been used with both airlines and airports at the other end of the route network with a view to introducing new services. Examples where such a proactive approach has led to the introduction of new services to Dublin, include the annual Icelandic charter services in autumn/winter, the new direct service to Helsinki, and the recently introduced direct Singapore Airlines 747 cargo service between Dublin and Singapore. Indeed, the latter service has been so successful that Singapore airlines have recently doubled the capacity on this route by adding a second weekly 747 service.

A Partnership Approach

Aer Rianta believes that airports can most effectively facilitate regional economic development by adopting a partnership approach with a very broad range of key interested parties. These include:

• airline customers;

• the travelling public;

- local communities;

- local authorities;

- tourism authorities;

- local chambers of commerce;

- airports at the other end of the route network.

The interests of all of these parties are interlinked to a significant degree, and the more these interests can be focused towards common goals, the more effective will be the outcome in terms of regional development.

INFRASTRUCTURAL DEVELOPMENTS

Because of the huge surge in passenger volumes (especially over the past three years when traffic has increased by 50 per cent), facilities have been stretched to capacity at Dublin Airport. Aer Rianta has in place a comprehensive development plan for Dublin Airport called *"Airport 1 – Creating the Best Airport"* which will involve investing £170 million in new facilities at Dublin Airport over a 5-year period. Many of the new projects have been completed, including the following.

- Multi-storey car parking complex (1996).

- Major new taxiway systems (1994-1996).

- Departure lounges in Pier A – Phase 1 (1995).

A large number of new projects are scheduled to be completed over the next few years. The principal ones are:

- new surface car-parking: 5,000 spaces (1997);

- departure lounges in Pier A – Phase 2 (1997);

- departure lounges in the old central terminal building (1997);

- new check-in area on Arrivals Road (1997);

- terminal extension/new Pier C (early 1998);

- new Great Southern Hotel at Dublin Airport (early 1998);

- additional apron/taxiway (1997/1998);

- main runway extension (1999);

- 6-bay extension of main terminal (2000).

These projects, when completed, will increase the capacity of the existing site at Dublin Airport to about 14 million passengers per annum with the possibility of additional expansion, if required, on the present site. The additional benefits derived from an investment programme of this magnitude include increased employment in the construction industry, extra spending power etc.

FUNDING AIRPORT DEVELOPMENT

All investment is funded from a combination of retained profits and (modest) borrowings. Aer Rianta has no recourse to the Exchequer for funding its investment programme. Indeed, over the past ten years, Aer Rianta has contributed over £134 million in dividends to the Exchequer.

The breakdown of Aer Rianta's revenues at Dublin Airport is as follows.

- Airport charges: 24.7%.
- Property and car park revenues: 19.7%.
- Retail Income: 55.6%.

THE IMPORTANCE OF DUTY FREE

It can be seen from the above, how important Duty Free revenues are to Aer Rianta. This year, for example, Dublin Duty Free will have a turnover of about £65 million, and will contribute over 70 per cent of the net profit at Dublin Airport. This contribution underpins the very generous traffic incentive scheme described earlier, and helps fund development plans.

This business directly employs about 300 people at Dublin Airport, and many more in supplier and associated services. It is proposed to abolish duty and tax-free sales within the EU with effect from 1 July 1999.

To give an indication of the scale of this business, which has been with us since 1947, the value of the total intra-EU duty and tax-free business is estimated to be worth about $6 billion, and to support about 140,000 jobs.

If intra-EU duty and tax-free selling is abolished, Ireland will be particularly hard-hit because the vast bulk of travel to and from Ireland is within the EU. The consequences are very serious, not just for Aer Rianta but also for airlines and ferries who depend significantly on duty free.

Among the consequences are the following.

- Significantly increased airport charges.

- Loss of direct revenue to airlines, both leading to higher air fares, (and higher ferry charges also) leading to lower number of passengers/tourists.

- Reduced ability to invest in facilities.

- Loss of jobs, with associated social consequences.

Aer Rianta's duty free shops both in Ireland and abroad act as an important 'window to the world' for many quality Irish products, such as whiskey/liqueurs, fashion and glass and giftware.

CONCLUSIONS

I'd like to briefly summarise how I see airports – and Dublin Airport in particular – facilitating regional economic growth. In summary, the critical factors influencing Dublin Airport in its facilitation of regional economic growth are as follows.

- Low-cost environment for our airline customers.

- A quest for excellence in customer service standards.

- Provision of high-quality airport facilities.

- Proactive development of market opportunities.

- Indefinite continuation of intra-EU duty and tax-free business.

DUBLIN'S GROWTH AT THE EXPENSE OF THE REGIONS

John Higgins

Acting Chief Executive
Western Development Commission

INTRODUCTION

As Dublin now prepares to install itself as the leading light of Irish tourism, issues may arise as to the effect this will have on the city, on the regions and on tourism in general.

The immediate question, which must be posed, is whether Ireland's booming tourism industry is to be allowed to follow the market trends of urban-led growth with the consequences this would have on the industry's relative market share for the regions. Should those who are empowered with promoting the sector try to ensure that the sector under threat for market share receives more specific treatment than that being provided to Dublin? Will Dublin's tourism growth not now continue without the incentives being applied under the operational programme, which is geared to suit the larger developments and investments? Should the current mid-term review of the programme not give serious consideration to changing the focus to assist the regions under threat for relative market share?

Examination of these issues must inevitably lead to scrutiny of the overall growth of Dublin, because it is impossible to disassociate the tourism sector from the matrix that is urban and rural growth.

FURTHER PARALYSIS

It is fair to say that Dublin city has incredible tourism potential. It is also true to state that of all the countries of Europe, Ireland has the greatest dispersal in the tourist industry in comparison to, for instance, the UK where 60 per cent of overseas tourist visits are concentrated in London. The cultural heritage that is Dublin's can indeed become a massive force for tourism development. The literary heritage of Joyce *et al* will reinforce this development, even though those Joycean scholars will willingly explain that James Joyce underlined the paralysis of the city centre and centralisation as a common thread through much of his works. It is this threatening paralysis of Dublin that will form the core of my analysis in this chapter.

THE CONTRIBUTION OF URBAN TOURISM

Major tourism developments in urban areas also benefit rural development through the following factors.

- The generation of added-value enterprises and sustainable employment in the regions.

- The attraction of tourists to rural hinterlands.

- The stimulation of secondary investment in tourism products and marketing in rural areas.

- Prompting action to protect and enhance the heritage of landscape, history and culture which is a major part of the tourist attraction.

REGIONAL GROWTH FROM TOURISM

Rural tourism is a powerful instrument of regional policy, assisting in raising incomes and providing employment in the country's poorer, and more remote, regions. It can bring economic activity and new opportunities to areas to which it may be difficult to attract industrial development. It can also energise and raise the morale of communities in the regions, many of which have been adversely affected by emigration and depopulation. In other words, tourism acts naturally as an instrument of regional balance in Ireland. Any efforts to distort this balance must be examined carefully by those who propose to support urban-led tourism whilst also purporting to care for balanced regional development.

Recent trends in per capita spending over the past five years are indeed a cause for concern. While the regions and the western seaboard has a high base of tourist spending, it is true to say that this market share is being gradually reduced, to the point that an examination of increases in per capita spend shows

Dublin and the eastern region having the greatest increase, while
the advantage of the western seaboard is being gradually whit-
tled away. This is something which Bord Fáilte must address,
and which the regions under threat must monitor carefully. The
regions must demand a restoration of the balance.

THE IDENTITY QUESTION

The move towards urban tourism as a leader in the development
of the sector must also be monitored from an identity perspective. If the environmentally green picture of Ireland is to be
maintained can this be best achieved through greater emphasis
on rural Ireland or on cities where too often the pollution of
rivers and carbon monoxide emission are a health and environmental hazard?

WHOSE EXPENSE?

Any move towards large-scale support for urban tourism must
examine these serious issues while also addressing the more
serious issue of introducing another growth factor into the
equation, of Dublin's growth pattern. The title of this chapter,
"Dublin's Growth at the Expense of the Regions" should be
amended to read "Dublin's Growth at Dublin's Expense and at
the Expense of the Regions". In other words, it is true to say
that the bulbous growth of Dublin, whereby its population has
grown from 720,000 in 1971 to 1.2 million in 1996 has been firstly at the expense of Dublin and latterly at the expense of the
regions. The deterioration in the quality of life for Dubliners
from this increase in population has led to the nightmare of
traffic congestion with its effect on the physical and mental
health of Dublin's citizens evidenced daily by an increase in
road rage incidents. Is Dublin to become a horn-blaring nightmare, equivalent to New York's Manhattan? This congestion
has also led to the other social nightmares, all of which combine
to reduce the quality of life of the citizens of this lovely city and
which make its streets unsafe, its rivers unclean, its roads
unfriendly and its people unsure. The cause of all this is the
greed of a few and the blindness of many (who have Dublin's
interest at heart) but who are suffering from tunnel vision.

Of course, this unstoppable momentum of growth that is the
Dublin of 1997 has also been at the expense of the regions, prin-

cipally at the expense of rural Ireland which has gradually been denuded of its population – a population which has been induced and dragged towards the prospects of high-tech jobs which are placed in Dublin and its periphery. Rural families are educating their children to such a high standard that they must leave to follow the high-tech jobs trail, a trail which need never have been created, if only this mismatching of job placements with the job skills on offer was not permitted by IDA Ireland. The recent decision to reintroduce a regional jobs policy in an effort to redress this pattern should be welcomed by all who care about Dublin and the regions.

URBAN/RURAL ALLIANCE FOR THE SAKE OF SANITY

The threat of urban growth is not just a threat for Dublin or of Dublin. It is just as much a threat in Galway, which is now the fastest growing city in Ireland. Like Dublin, Galway must also be careful. Further controls need to be put in place immediately or the "City of the Tribes" will find itself with more tribal warfare on its streets than mediaeval Galway ever witnessed. Urban crime and attacks on tourists and visitors are becoming just as much of a feature in Galway as in Dublin.

THE SANE SOLUTION

A three-track approach should be considered in the context of a solution.

Track 1

The formation of an Urban/Rural Alliance working towards the reduction of urban sprawl and urban growth, which will put a halt to rural depopulation and which will support a policy of dispersal of development for the common good. Every modern economy seeks to pursue these objectives. In a small modern economy, such as Ireland, the achievement of these objectives, while being patently desirable, are also easily attainable. Dublin, Galway and the other urban centres must stop flexing their mighty muscles – political muscles, business muscles, monied muscles – must let go of the policies that are choking these cities to death, must arrest the headlong rush of agglomeration and congestion and must plan now to participate in a natural growth process. With just 2,800 acres of new housing land left in Dublin, the need to carefully plan for the next generation of Dubliners is a priority. Otherwise, the next generation of Dubliners will be forced to leave their native city and like so many generations of country-folk will be forced to live away from their place of birth.

Track 2

In response to the key recommendations in the Action Plan for Western Development, which inspired the establishment of the Western Development Commission, the government has requested the NESC (Natural Economic and Social Council) to prepare a report on population settlement patterns. This report will analyse the trends in settlement patterns, examine its causes and will make recommendations for future policy.

Track 3

I propose that the government should plan for dispersal of development, starting now. To pursue such a policy makes strong social and economic sense. Growth strategies should be geared towards the three inter-linked approaches of:

- natural growth areas;
- incentivised growth areas;
- artificial growth areas.

Natural Growth Areas
In which urban areas are allowed to grow naturally. This implies not attracting more people to move to urban areas, and involves the entire removal of any incentives, which accelerate the momentum towards centralisation or agglomeration. It also involves the end of re-zoning on the periphery of Dublin. Intense planning for the real social and economic needs of Dublin should accompany this approach.

Incentivised Growth Areas
To be supported using incentives to entice people to move to smaller towns and to rural areas outside the 'halo' of the five main urban centres. This approach will involve further decen-tralisation of business by incentives and a planned programme to spread the employment provided in government departments and agencies across the entire country.

Artificial Growth Areas

Whereby new population centres are planned and spread uniformly across the entire country. The effect of this latter approach would mean that instead of building another new centre adjoining Athlone, Ballina, Tuam, Buncrana, each artificial growth area will be carefully planned and provided for, so avoiding the negative impact, which was experienced in the early years of Tallaght and Blanchardstown.

The emphasis in any future application of EU structural funds should endeavour to support these approaches.

CONCLUSION

A reasonable debate on the real needs of Dublin needs to be instigated. Is it not fair to support the case that Dublin should have a special action plan for its development – a plan which will approach the task not from the narrow viewpoint of an economic rate of return; but which will focus on social considerations, on methods to preserve the quality of life of Dublin, on schemes to restore and protect the environment of the city and on ways to ensure that jobs are provided, which meet the skillbase and the needs of the natural population of Dublin. To prepare such a plan is a mammoth task for the geographer, the sociologist and the economist working in tandem with Dublin Corporation and the various other local authorities within a 25 mile radius of the city. To support such a plan demands foresight and vision, and above all political courage from our leaders who are too often disinclined to see beyond the horizon of the next election.

In planning for this change and in seeking the courage to support it perhaps the words of Machiavelli will inspire courage while instilling caution.

There is nothing more difficult to take in hand, more perilous to conduct, or more uncertain in its success, than to take the lead in the introduction of a new order of things, because the innovator has for enemies all those who have done well under the old conditions and lukewarm defenders in those who may do well under the new.

TOURISM AND THE PROPERTY SECTOR

Phil Reilly

Monarch Properties

COMPANY BACKGROUND

Monarch Properties has been in property development and management for the past 25 years. The company was initially set up in Dundalk as a building contractor but moved into industrial development and subsequently entered into the construction of shopping centres. Monarch have developed retail schemes in Dundalk, Athlone, Navan and Drogheda as well as projects in Finglas, Nutgrove and The Square in Tallaght, which is Ireland's largest shopping centre in excess of 0.5 million square feet.

In early 1997, Monarch completed a multiplex cinema complex in Manchester in the Nyex complex. Two major projects under recent construction were Bloomfields, Dun Laoghaire, a new shopping and leisure complex costing £20 million which opened in May 1997 and a new town centre shopping development in Llanelli in South Wales also costing £20 million which opened in November 1997.

Monarch have also completed two leisure developments for United Cinemas International at Malahide Road in Coolock and The Square in Tallaght which is the most successful of UCI's cinemas in Europe. It attracts over 30,000 customers per week which has peaked at a record 52,000 customers, beating a large complex in Dusseldorf which has six more screens than Tallaght.

THE BUSINESS OF TOURISM: URBAN-LED ENOUGH?

The Square in Tallaght which opened in 1990 falls under the Monarch banner. Visitors to The Square will see many innovative services and facilities such as a permanent stage, permanent exhibition area, 2FM radio station, customer service desk, crèche and many other facilities.

Approximately 14 million customers visit the centre per annum and Monarch have become actively involved in the tourist business in retailing by developing overseas coach shopping trips to The Square from north Wales and England which peak at eighteen tours per week during the summer period. These coach tours, which have been operating for the past three years, are provided with a discount book for use throughout the shopping centre, a discounted breakfast, a tour of Glendalough, or Ballykissangel, and some more shopping in the city centre prior to their return by the HSS super ferry.

Apart from these overseas tours, Monarch encourage Irish-based tours throughout the year and again these peak during the summer period with the school tours and special interest groups. The Square also enjoys a share of the 4,000 Icelandic visitors who come to Dublin in November/December each year. The Square has a fully fledged tourist office which is operated by Dublin Tourism and was set up with the local authority – South Dublin County Council – partially funded by the landlord.

The design of the centre allows major functions to be held in the central area. For example, in March 1997, the Circuit of Ireland Rally was based at The Square. This is a typical example of the active involvement of the centre management in promoting the region and this event was organised in conjunction with the South Dublin County Council, the Chamber of Commerce and the Abberley Court Hotel.

BLOOMFIELDS SHOPPING CENTRE, DUN LAOGHAIRE

Bloomfields Shopping Centre opened in May 1997. This is a new concept supermarket which is anchored by Tesco and it comprises another 25 shop units, 12 screen multiplex cinema, apartments and 550 car spaces. Part of the development has an Arts Centre which is utilised by the very active arts community in Dun Laoghaire.

The site for this development was formerly the Dominican Convent and includes a small oratory which was constructed in the grounds of the convent in about 1920. This oratory building was donated by a local parishioner as a thanksgiving for peace after the First World War. The oratory although architecturally unimposing from the exterior, is renowned for the marvellous interior decoration by Sister Concepta Lynch who worked on decorating the oratory from 1920 to 1936 with motifs from Irish medieval illuminated manuscripts. The oratory also contains seven excellent stained glass windows by the renowned artist Harry Clarke.

Monarch received a support grant for restoration from the European Commission whereby the building and its surrounds will be handed over by Monarch to construct a structure to encase the oratory and to preserve the building and to also provide an information centre.

The shopping centre restaurant, gardens and courtyard are located next to the oratory. It is intended to use this feature as a marketing tool to promote the Bloomfields development linking it, for instance, to the Stena Line for overseas visitors, school tours, special interest groups and tourists generally from throughout Ireland, the UK and worldwide.

THE VALE, TRALEE

The Vale is part of the Lee Valley Development which is the latest in a series of ambitious tourism-related developments to be undertaken by Tralee Urban District Council in conjunction with Shannon Development and other State agencies as well as local community and business interests.

This 20-acre site lies on the southern side of Tralee and extends along the Lee Valley on the main Tralee/Dingle road from Ballymullen in the east to Blennerville in the west. The site has a frontage of 950 metres and is within 500 metres of Tralee town centre and extends from the N70 in the east to the Aqua Dome which is a £6 million water/leisure development which opened in 1995 and attracts over 200,000 visitors per year. Five acres of the property are designated under the Urban Renewal Act and these lands qualify for a package of attractive tax incentives.

As part of Monarch's bid for selection, consideration had to be given to the potential and quality of the surrounding area. The project includes the following attractions.

• A hotel and conference centre.

• Hotel apartments.

• Holiday apartments.

• A themed retail village which will incorporate a themed public house/restaurant.

- A multi-purpose leisure box.

- A tourist service centre.

This proposed development is highly compatible with the general tourism/leisure/amenity designation of the Lee Valley and Tralee area. The entire development consists of a mix of tourist accommodation and indoor and outdoor recreation facilities.

The Vale will provide additional accommodation and attractions for the large influx of yearly visitors to Tralee which is estimated at 500,000 per annum.

Hotel Development

In order to accommodate this influx, the first part of the development will be a 110-bedroom hotel with restaurant and small business facilities. The accommodation will mainly target the budget end of the tourist market. The approximate area of this development is three acres.

In addition to standard bedrooms, 48 hotel apartments will also be provided. Customers using the hotel or hotel apartments will have the choice of accommodation, i.e. the traditional hotel accommodation services etc. or self-catering apartments but with the option of using hotel facilities if desired.

Self-catering Accommodation

A second part of this scheme includes 84 self-catering, 2-bedroom apartments which we intend will have a 4-star rating in accordance with the requirements laid down by Bord Fáilte. These units will be designed with traditional Irish features with quite a bit of stone on the facade, two bedrooms, living/dining area, fully fitted kitchen, two bathrooms and an open fire place. They will be fully equipped and will include a welcome pack, including tea, butter and sugar, for the first night's stay.

Themed Retail Village

The third part of this development is the themed retail village outlet which as earlier stated, will include a pub/restaurant of approximately 10,000 square feet, 12/13 smaller craft type units and a 1,400 square metre outlet which will provide tourists with a destination for shopping.

Monarch propose to theme this building on an old Irish railway station and the reason for this is that it is also intended to extend the steam engine railway track from Blennerville which currently stops at the aqua dome into the themed village. A number of operators have been identified including one UK retailer who specialises in this type of themed retailing.

A heavy emphasis will be placed on coach facilities and good parking. It can be noted that we have approximately 200 car spaces immediately adjoining this village and we have five set down stops for coaches. Within the overall complex we can accommodate approximately twenty coaches. Most provincial towns in Ireland, including Tralee, have difficulty in providing parking and easy access for coaches.

It will also include a fairly large pub/restaurant facility which will have the ability to cater for three or four coaches at a time at lunch times or other peak times. This element of the development will be situated on three acres and is intended to encourage combined shopping trips and leisure and tourism.

Leisure Box

The multi-purpose leisure box is a 6,000 square metre building which will have a main auditorium with two side wings which are dedicated to catering for major events. It will also be linked to the adjoining hotel and will have the ability to house conferences for up to 3,000 delegates, sit down concerts for about the same number of people, exhibitions and sports events. It is intended to house at least two major themed events during the year, which will not compete with the Rose of Tralee but will compliment the tourist offer in Tralee and Kerry particularly during off peak times during the season. The building will include state of the art facilities including television and radio links to our national radio and television stations and will also have multi-lingual facilities with the most modern, up to date audio and video equipment necessary for conferences.

Tourist Service Centre

The final part of the development is the tourist service centre. This will comprise of petrol filling station, small mini-market, a medical centre with dentist and doctor, a late-hour pharmacy, a car rental outlet, a small repair area for breakdowns and a drive-thru restaurant. This facility should be extensively used at peak times for all types of mishaps and emergencies.

Overall, this is a mixed development specifically designed for the tourist market in an urban area. One other key element, which is very important to the future success of this development, is an overall management package which will require each operator in this development to participate in a common marketing strategy. Monarch propose to set up a management company who will provide the usual house-keeping services (cleaning, security, maintenance, upkeep) but will also retain the services of a marketing manager who will actively market the project with the other agencies in Kerry and Ireland.

It is intended that a typical visitor to this particular scheme would have a number of choices of accommodation, restaurants or pubs whether it is the hotel or the themed pub or indeed the drive-thru restaurant. He/she will have the option of using the very fine aqua dome, will have the facility for shopping, including different types of shopping for crafts and very good Irish produce. The multi-purpose leisure box will be used to anchor the scheme and to attract visitors not only to this particular development but to the Tralee area in general.

The Vale tourism and leisure scheme will highlight the facilities on offer in the development and will also package the adjoining major tourist attractions of the Blennerville Mill, the new Jeanie Johnston ship costing £6 million, the internationally famous Siamsa Tire, the national folk theatre of Ireland, the Ash Memorial Hall and, of course, Tralee with its excellent restaurants, very fine pubs and good traditional shopping.

Kerry is famous for its golf courses, fishing, shooting and walks. Tralee also has a greyhound track which is being revamped at a cost of over £3 million as well an excellent race track. There is a lot for somebody coming to The Vale which is within an urban area in a rural area.

These examples give a flavour of the developer's perspective in what Monarch are trying to achieve. Monarch's role as developers is to feed a need. This type of development offers choice and variety which would not necessarily be available in a stand alone tourist centre in a rural area.

THE ESSENTIALS FOR SUCCESS

John Kelly
AIB Bank

INTRODUCTION

Tourism is arguably Ireland's most dynamic industry. The facts speak for themselves particularly in relation to the increase in the number of visitors coming to this country and the revenue generated. It is reckoned that £4 in every £100 spent here is spent by tourists and, in terms of job creation, it is estimated that one in every three new jobs created in the country since 1988 is in some way related to tourism activities. In this respect tourism is vital because it has the ability to create and sustain jobs in parts of the country where other job and wealth creation opportunities can be limited. It is also estimated that the exchequer benefits to the tune of IR£1 billion per annum in terms of VAT, excise duties, etc. on the money spent by tourists.

FACTORS OF SUCCESS FOR IRISH TOURISM

Undoubtedly there have been a number of key drivers for growth including the fact that 'to be Irish' is currently very fashionable. This 'fashionability' of Ireland is due to a number of factors some of which include Irish success abroad in the fields of art, music, culture and sport. During the first ceasefire in Northern Ireland, an increased number of visitors from the UK were attracted to Ireland.

The Celtic Tiger has put more money in people's pockets and an increasing number of Irish people now have the financial capability to enjoy short breaks and weekend holidays apart from the annual two-three week vacation. Another key driver for growth includes the upward trend in special interest holidays particularly focused around sporting, cultural activities and hobbies. Bord Fáilte has changed its style, its marketing strategy and its focus but it takes a while for the benefits to flow through.

BUSINESS TOURISM

The issue of business tourism cannot be ignored and the ever increasing number of multinationals who are choosing Ireland as an investment location is helping to support the increasing numbers travelling through our air and ferry ports on business travel. In AIB headquarters in Ballsbridge, for example, hardly a day goes by without 20 or 30 colleagues from our subsidiaries abroad being in Dublin for business of one kind or another. Another key driver for growth includes the mobility of international conferences and there is ample evidence to suggest that Ireland is getting its fair share of such conferences. What a difference a national conference centre would make to the obvious potential within this lucrative market.

SUSTAINING THE GROWTH PROCESS

The key factors can be summarised as follows.

1. For businesses in the tourist industry to survive and prosper, they need certainty: certainty as to politics, interest and exchange rates. The economic history books will show that economic growth in Ireland was achieved in the periods of sustained single digit interest rates similar to those we are enjoying at the moment. Low interest rates give investment activity its incentive. Our 'obsession' in Ireland with tax and property, when combined, provides a potent cocktail to motivate investment intention. The success of some of the designated seaside resorts, the IFSC, Temple Bar and indeed the overall benefit brought about by urban renewal schemes demonstrates this.

2. Marketing Ireland is not a battle of products but a battle of perceptions. We currently enjoy the perception of being clean, green and friendly – in other words a nice place to visit. It is only when you travel abroad that you appreciate the natural asset that Ireland has to offer in terms of its environment.

3. There are a number of institutions, associations and organisations working at the forefront of the tourism industry. There is an onus on all of us to take time out and listen to the feedback from people such as the Irish Hotel Federation, CERT, Bord Fáilte. We constantly need to be re-evaluating the needs of our customers, finding out what they want and putting in place the necessary measures that are required to meet their

needs. Sustaining growth can also be achieved with more support from the centre. The combination of tax and property incentives is a powerful way of accelerating further development in the tourism infrastructure. More fertile thinking from the centre around such areas as seaside resorts, urban relief and similar type schemes will in my opinion, motivate, increased investment in this sector.

4. As bankers we are asked from time to time what the characteristics of successful tourism projects are. While there is no precise template, I believe successful tourism projects share some or all of the following characteristics. In general, tourism projects tend to be started by people who have gained in experience or expertise within the industry prior to initiating their own business. Many fine projects have been started by people who spotted a gap in the market when they were employed by someone else. This trend appears to be particularly prevalent in the hotel and public house sectors. Running a tourism business requires a high level of personal energy and enthusiasm. Unlike running a manufacturing or a service industry with traditional working hours, the tourism industry is unique in that it requires you or your staff to provide a service almost round the clock. Dealing with visitors particularly in the accommodation business requires a high level of dedication and patience and in general also requires working an extraordinary number of unsociable hours. Successful business practitioners in this sector also tend to be able to establish key relationships and a focused network with people who can help them achieve their objectives. All around the country for example there appears to be an informal network between owner/managers of bed and breakfast facilities.

Why, for example, do coaches stop at one restaurant or heritage centre in preference to others? It is probably because the owner/manager of the restaurant or the heritage centre has established a good working relationship with the coach or tour operator. Business practitioners in the tourism industry are generally well-informed. They take time out to attend conferences to learn about the macro issues or simply to network with other people within the same industry to establish issues and challenges that are arising at local, regional or national level. To be forewarned is to be forearmed and the availability of relevant information and data on the dynamics of the industry does help practitioners in the operational and strategic planning aspects of their business. Amateurs in business have the odds stacked against them. In general we have found within AIB that successful business practitioners show no reluctance to buy in whatever expertise is required to enhance their business prospects.

As an owner/manager of a business it is impossible to be an expert in all areas such as marketing, taxation, business planning, etc. Successful practitioners know their weaknesses and buy in at an early stage whatever expertise it takes to plug any obvious gap in the skills and management areas. Finally, we have found within AIB that successful business practitioners are quick to identify early warning signs and to take corrective action or make adjustments to minimise their vulnerability in a business downturn.

THREATS TO SUCCESS

Some of the early warning signs, which business practitioners in the tourism industry should look out for, include a general weakening of the economy both at home and abroad. We all know too well the sensitivity of Irish tourism, the US$/IR£ exchange rate or indeed the Stg/IR£ exchange rate. Some of the early warning signs that bankers look for in reviewing credit applications from projects in the tourist industry include a downward trend in the occupancy levels, staff mobility, failure to comply with health and safety regulations, poor local/national press, etc.

Some of the red lights on dashboard include poor financial planning, particularly with cost overruns on construction or refurbishment of premises. A sudden focus on a new niche market is also an early warning sign because when we experience a downturn in our business we tend to look for a quick fix in the hope that we can plug an income leakage or a fall in profits. A sudden focus on a new market, without adequate research and back-up information, frequently only compounds the problem. Other warning signs include frequent unscheduled requests for unusual facilities not in line with projections or more importantly owners who distance themselves from the business.

On the other hand, some of the key characteristics for successful loan applications are as follows. A business plan is required as a precondition. Business plans should demonstrate evidence of market research, analysis of competitors and a sensitivity analysis with the financial figures based on lower sales and/or pricing levels. Ideally, the promoter should demonstrate his/her ability to have contingencies to deal with cost overruns particularly in relation to major capex programmes.

FINANCING PROPOSALS

There is a rough rule of thumb for start-up projects in terms of how the proposal should be financed. In essence, the rule proposes a third, a third and a third concept in that a third of the project should be financed with bank debt, a third with grants and a third with promoter's equity and/or retained profits. This rule of thumb lends itself to equal risk sharing for all parties concerned particularly in a less benign economy. For existing projects seeking monies for expansion, I believe that the debt/equity ratio should be in the region of 60 per cent/65 per cent and that projected profit after tax should be greater or equal to 2.5 times the proposed interest bill. In terms of supporting your project, the security level should be at a minimal level of 1.25 times.

One of the major changes coming down the tracks which will have an impact on tourist projects is the single European currency. In AIB we believe that the overall impact of the euro will be positive. We believe it will motivate an increased volume of traffic from the euro countries because the presence of a stable, fixed exchange rate is of particular significance to this industry as many foreign exchange transactions tend to be high volume/low value.

There will be an operational impact for retailers as regards being ready to facilitate the acceptance of the euro as legal tender. In simple terms, when the euro becomes a reality we will all need to make changes to tangible items such as cash registers, software, invoices, etc. The arrival of the euro also promises a more stable interest rate environment which should help provide more certainty and stability as regarding planning for the future. The availability of stable interest rates appears to be a key ingredient in terms of motivating investment in this country. One word of caution, however, relates to the fact that the euro could advance without the participation of the UK in the early stages. This obviously could make sterling vulnerable to volatile exchange rates which in turn could either help to improve or neutralise the competitiveness of Ireland vis à vis the British tourist.

AIB Bank is keen to support national economic objectives by supporting tourism which we view as a key performing sector of the economy. Strategically we earmarked this sector for special attention three years ago and we believe we have provided a number of innovative and unique schemes to help support our customers around the country. We have a number of dedicated specialists within our lending system who work exclusively on tourist-related projects, with particular regard to accommodation. We also have a range of affinity schemes and a number of special purpose publications all of which are available at any AIB branch. When it comes to dealing with tourist projects we are not cavalier, we do not pretend to have all the answers but we welcome a challenge in terms of helping the promoter find the optimum financing mix or provide an innovative solution to a financial problem. We would welcome the opportunity to discuss the requirements of any new or existing player in the industry and in this regard the reality for us is "if you are in business – then we are in business".

TOURISM PROJECTS: THE ECONOMIC CONTRIBUTION TO REGENERATION

Dr D R Vaughan

Bournemouth University

INTRODUCTION

It is the opportunities, and in particular the demonstration through research of the economic opportunities, that tourism offers for urban regeneration, that forms the focus of this chapter. A selection of 'advocacy' data is presented, which shows that tourism development is worthwhile in terms of the scale and quality of benefits offered. This chapter does not argue that tourism is, or should be, the only vehicle for regeneration, but that it can make a worthwhile contribution. This chapter has three main parts.

- The first looks at the problem of measuring the impacts of tourism developments.

- The second part details the economic benefits of cultural tourism in Merseyside in 1985.

- The third examines the benefits provided by three different tourism developments which have been supported through the inner city grant aid regime(s).

THE URBAN POLICY CONTEXT

Since the 1960s, the UK has operated a range of urban regeneration policies, many of which still operate today in a similar or revised form. These policies are both defensive, attempting to stop the decline of the urban area, and active, attempting to promote the growth of the urban area. There have been:

a) *traditional urban policies*, such as Special Development Areas status, the provision of advance factories and training schemes;

attractors and enhancers has taken place for many years in an unco-ordinated fashion (many of those developments have formed the basis of the strategies), what has been different over the last fifteen years is that urban areas have been 'designing' their product they offer (Law, 1994, p. 9). Thus, while most urban areas have focused on conferences and exhibitions at the business end of the urban offer, at the leisure end a focus on, for example, culture (Birmingham) and on sports (Sheffield) can be observed.

The Nature and Classification of the Impacts

The development of the attractors and enhancers has been the focus of tourism strategies for regenerating urban areas. Identifying the impacts of these strategies, or specific developments within the strategies, is problematic and wide ranging given the diversity of those impacts. As an example consider the classification system in Table 9.1.

Table 9.1: Classifying the Benefits and Costs of a Tourism Development

Benefits/costs	Classification of Impacts		
	Primary Examples of impacts	Secondary Examples of impacts	Tertiary Examples of impacts
Economic benefit Economic cost	Jobs at the project Refurbishment cost	Spending in the area Job displacement	Image
Social benefit	More facilities	Business viability	Changing attitudes
Social cost	Grant diversion	Retail displacement	
Environmental benefit Environmental cost	Refurbishment Disruption	Improvement catalyst Increased traffic	Visual Amenity

b) *inner city policies*; such as Partnership Area status, the creation of economic development offices and the designation of Industrial Improvement Areas;

c) *Urban Programme policies*; such as Urban Development Corporations, Enterprise Zones and Urban Development Grant;

d) *European Union policies*, such as the European Regional Development Grant and the Social Fund.

THE TOURISM COMPONENT

In the 1980s, tourism (and its associated activities such as the arts, sport, the heritage, entertainment, etc.) began to feature in the strategic and tactical activities of the authorities responsible for urban areas, for example Bradford, in respect of these urban policy tools. This use of tourism in relation to urban regeneration arose because tourism was identified as being a growth industry offering complementarity with the following areas.

- Other activities that were sought after by visitors: both those that might act as attractors (the arts, sport, etc.) and those that might act as enhancers of the visitor experience (shops, transport, restaurants). Thus tourism development offered the opportunity to increase the viability of other activities and to maintain a more substantial range of opportunities for local residents in declining areas.

- The environment and in respect of which tourism could be seen as a catalyst to environmental improvement both in terms of the general physical condition of the area and in relation to specific buildings and areas which, having lost their original purpose, might take on a new role.

- The need to present a 'new' image to the world and to remove the negative connotations of urban areas with social and physical degeneration so that such areas became more attractive to other inward investment.

- With the overall objective of increasing economic activity in that tourism offered the benefits of increased business turnover, increased local income and jobs at a possibly 'lower' cost and at a quicker speed, than the more traditional forms of economic regeneration.

During the 1980s, these opportunities offered by tourism formed the basis of strategies developed in different urban areas, for example Merseyside (DRV Research 1986), and were presented in the English Tourist Board 'roadshow' on "Vision for the Cities" in 1989/90. The proposition of these strategic appraisals was that tourism offered major opportunities for urban regeneration.

Looking back it is, therefore, a surprisingly short time-scale over which tourism has been developed as a vehicle for urban regeneration, in most, if not all, major urban areas in the UK. This development has often been in the face of criticism about the quality of what was offered by tourism and a view that real development could only be achieved through manufacturing (Law, 1994, p. 3). However, over the last fifteen years tourism has been a major element in, for example, the regeneration strategies of Birmingham, Manchester, Sheffield, Glasgow, etc. It is not that urban areas had not used or developed urban-based attractions before, for example the Edinburgh Festival (Vaughan, 1977). It is that prior to the last fifteen years "little time or finance were put into this…(development of)…the resource base for tourism" (Law, 1994, p. 3) and, therefore, the scale of the effort and the co-ordination of the effort in urban areas over the last fifteen years has been different.

THE POLICY IMPLEMENTATION

The way in which urban policy has been implemented over the last fifteen years has been identified by Law (1994, pp. 24-25). He has identified the key elements that, while generally applicable to all types of urban regeneration strategy in the UK, have been equally applicable in the tourism context. These are:

- an emphasis on economic objectives;

- an emphasis on obtaining private investment as part of the development funding and the growth of public-private partnerships;

- semi-autonomous public agencies to 'drive' the development, with the public sector being responsible for anchors to draw people in and for infrastructure;

- a focus on the inner city, emphasising property development, flagship projects and image improvement.

MEASURING THE IMPACT OF TOURISM

The Types of Tourism in Urban Areas

Urban areas attract three different types of tourist the di being the motivation for the visit.

1. *Business visitors*: business, conferences, meetings an tions.

2. *Pleasure visitors*: long stay, short stay or day trip.

3. *Visitors to friends and relations.*

The Components of the Tourism Product

These urban tourists are attracted by, and or servic facilities and opportunities offered within the urban a can broadly be divided into two categories.

1. *Urban attractors*: for example, events (conferences, and festivals), the urban landscape (the architec spaces), the culture (museums, art galleries, live arts) and sport.

2. *Urban enhancers*: for example, the visit infrastruct modation, shops, restaurants), the travel inf (access, internal travel, parking) and the visitor in (TICs, guides, signposts).

The difference between the two is that normally th will motivate potential tourists to visit the urban ar enhancers, while important for the overall exp unlikely to be the reason for the visit. However, the not be as clear cut as this. In certain circum enhancers may also motivate a visit, for example a ping environment. In other circumstances, for some itors, the attractors will enhance the enjoyment o offering a range of possibilities in addition to the m tor for the visit (for example, the night-life offere performing arts).

What has been different over the last fifteen urban areas, through their urban regeneration st been attempting to position themselves within th Thus, while the development of those elements

b) *inner city policies*; such as Partnership Area status, the creation of economic development offices and the designation of Industrial Improvement Areas;

c) *Urban Programme policies*; such as Urban Development Corporations, Enterprise Zones and Urban Development Grant;

d) *European Union policies*, such as the European Regional Development Grant and the Social Fund.

THE TOURISM COMPONENT

In the 1980s, tourism (and its associated activities such as the arts, sport, the heritage, entertainment, etc.) began to feature in the strategic and tactical activities of the authorities responsible for urban areas, for example Bradford, in respect of these urban policy tools. This use of tourism in relation to urban regeneration arose because tourism was identified as being a growth industry offering complementarity with the following areas.

- Other activities that were sought after by visitors: both those that might act as attractors (the arts, sport, etc.) and those that might act as enhancers of the visitor experience (shops, transport, restaurants). Thus tourism development offered the opportunity to increase the viability of other activities and to maintain a more substantial range of opportunities for local residents in declining areas.

- The environment and in respect of which tourism could be seen as a catalyst to environmental improvement both in terms of the general physical condition of the area and in relation to specific buildings and areas which, having lost their original purpose, might take on a new role.

- The need to present a 'new' image to the world and to remove the negative connotations of urban areas with social and physical degeneration so that such areas became more attractive to other inward investment.

- With the overall objective of increasing economic activity in that tourism offered the benefits of increased business turnover, increased local income and jobs at a possibly 'lower' cost and at a quicker speed, than the more traditional forms of economic regeneration.

During the 1980s, these opportunities offered by tourism formed the basis of strategies developed in different urban areas, for example Merseyside (DRV Research 1986), and were presented in the English Tourist Board 'roadshow' on "Vision for the Cities" in 1989/90. The proposition of these strategic appraisals was that tourism offered major opportunities for urban regeneration.

Looking back it is, therefore, a surprisingly short time-scale over which tourism has been developed as a vehicle for urban regeneration, in most, if not all, major urban areas in the UK. This development has often been in the face of criticism about the quality of what was offered by tourism and a view that real development could only be achieved through manufacturing (Law, 1994, p. 3). However, over the last fifteen years tourism has been a major element in, for example, the regeneration strategies of Birmingham, Manchester, Sheffield, Glasgow, etc. It is not that urban areas had not used or developed urban-based attractions before, for example the Edinburgh Festival (Vaughan, 1977). It is that prior to the last fifteen years "little time or finance were put into this...(development of)...the resource base for tourism" (Law, 1994, p. 3) and, therefore, the scale of the effort and the co-ordination of the effort in urban areas over the last fifteen years has been different.

THE POLICY IMPLEMENTATION

The way in which urban policy has been implemented over the last fifteen years has been identified by Law (1994, pp. 24-25). He has identified the key elements that, while generally applicable to all types of urban regeneration strategy in the UK, have been equally applicable in the tourism context. These are:

- an emphasis on economic objectives;

- an emphasis on obtaining private investment as part of the development funding and the growth of public-private partnerships;

- semi-autonomous public agencies to 'drive' the development, with the public sector being responsible for anchors to draw people in and for infrastructure;

- a focus on the inner city, emphasising property development, flagship projects and image improvement.

MEASURING THE IMPACT OF TOURISM

The Types of Tourism in Urban Areas

Urban areas attract three different types of tourist the difference being the motivation for the visit.

1. *Business visitors*: business, conferences, meetings and exhibitions.

2. *Pleasure visitors*: long stay, short stay or day trip.

3. *Visitors to friends and relations*.

The Components of the Tourism Product

These urban tourists are attracted by, and or serviced by, the facilities and opportunities offered within the urban area. These can broadly be divided into two categories.

1. *Urban attractors*: for example, events (conferences, exhibitions and festivals), the urban landscape (the architecture, open spaces), the culture (museums, art galleries, live performing arts) and sport.

2. *Urban enhancers*: for example, the visit infrastructure (accommodation, shops, restaurants), the travel infrastructure (access, internal travel, parking) and the visitor infrastructure (TICs, guides, signposts).

The difference between the two is that normally the attractors will motivate potential tourists to visit the urban area while the enhancers, while important for the overall experience, are unlikely to be the reason for the visit. However, the reality may not be as clear cut as this. In certain circumstances, the enhancers may also motivate a visit, for example a certain shopping environment. In other circumstances, for some types of visitors, the attractors will enhance the enjoyment of the visit by offering a range of possibilities in addition to the motivating factor for the visit (for example, the night-life offered by the live performing arts).

What has been different over the last fifteen years is that urban areas, through their urban regeneration strategies, have been attempting to position themselves within the marketplace. Thus, while the development of those elements referred to as attractors and enhancers has taken place for many years in an unco-ordinated fashion (many of those developments have formed the basis of the strategies), what has been different over the last fifteen years is that urban areas have been 'designing' their product they offer (Law, 1994, p. 9). Thus, while most urban areas have focused on conferences and exhibitions at the business end of the urban offer, at the leisure end a focus on, for example, culture (Birmingham) and on sports (Sheffield) can be observed.

The Nature and Classification of the Impacts

The development of the attractors and enhancers has been the focus of tourism strategies for regenerating urban areas. Identifying the impacts of these strategies, or specific developments within the strategies, is problematic and wide ranging given the diversity of those impacts. As an example consider the classification system in Table 9.1.

Table 9.1: Classifying the Benefits and Costs of a Tourism Development

Benefits/costs	Classification of Impacts		
	Primary Examples of impacts	Secondary Examples of impacts	Tertiary Examplesof impacts
Economic benefit Economic cost	Jobs at the project Refurbishment cost	Spending in the area Job displacement	Image
Social benefit	More facilities	Business viability	Changing attitudes
Social cost	Grant diversion	Retail displacement	
Environmental benefit Environmental cost	Refurbishment Disruption	Improvement catalyst Increased traffic	Visual Amenity

In Table 9.1, which is based on the Albert Dock development in Liverpool:

a) the primary impacts are those arising directly from the development and operation of the site;

b) the secondary impacts are those that arise elsewhere within the urban area as visitors to the site make use of, or require the development of, other parts of the urban economy;

c) the tertiary impacts are those which have no monetary value attached to them but which are attributable to the development.

The Basis of the Economic Impacts

It is not possible to go into each element of this classification in a chapter of this length. Therefore, this chapter focuses on the economic benefits of urban tourism developments. These economic benefits of tourism can arise in two ways.

1. Investment, either through spending on the development of new tourism-related facilities or activities or through the upgrading of existing facilities and activities.

2. The recurrent spending by visitors during the course of their visits.

The studies of the economic benefits of tourism have, by and large, focused on the recurrent spending as the investment element, while important, has largely been considered to be transient and the means to an end, which was increased by visitor spending.

The Phases of Economic Impact

The studies of the economic benefits of visitor spending have focused on the following four phases of impact.

1. The actual spending by visitors.

2. The direct impact of visitor spending on the local community through the incomes paid out by, and the jobs supported in, the businesses in which visitors spent their money.

3. The indirect impact of visitor spending on the local commu-

nity, through incomes and jobs, as a result of the businesses in which visitors spent their money purchasing goods and services from the local community.

4. The induced impact of visitor spending on the local community, through incomes and jobs, as a result of residents of the community spending the incomes they earned as a result of visitor spending.

The Focus of the Impact Measurements

The analyses of these four phases have focused on estimating:

- the total scale of the impacts and the phase in which they occurred, for example the total amount spent by visitors and the total number of jobs that resulted in the direct, indirect and induced phases of visitor spending;

- the rate of the impacts, for example the jobs supported per £10,000 spent by visitors or the jobs created per 10,000 visitor days;

- the distribution of the direct impacts, for example the proportion of jobs that were all-year and the proportion that were seasonal.

Complications in Measuring the Impacts

The basic method adopted in measuring the economic benefits resulting from visitor spending has been 'proportional multiplier analysis'. However, when assessing the impacts of tourism strategies and tactics, rather than simply measuring the scale and composition of the economic impacts of visitor spending, there are further complications. These additional complications arise when evaluating the use of public funds in tourism-related developments because consideration needs to be given to the extent to which the development is adding 'new' and additional benefits. This requires consideration of additionality, displacement, trade creation and the catalytic nature of the development.

- The level of additionality is dependent on whether the development would, or would not, have gone ahead without the public funds.

- The degree of displacement is dependent on whether the development has simply shifted activities between locations.

- The level of trade creation will depend on whether the spending in the local community by the visitors would have been made regardless of whether the development was there or not. (In some instances, it may also be appropriate to consider trade diversion if it is considered that the development is such that it may be putting off some potential tourists from visiting.)

- As indicated earlier, tourism-related developments will have both primary and secondary impacts. When evaluating tourism developments it is vital to include the secondary impacts or the true 'worth' of the development to the urban area will not be known.

THE IMPACTS OF URBAN TOURISM

The Scale of the Impacts

While it may seem improbable now, acceptance of the possible scale of tourism to cities, and by implication the scale of the economic impacts, was not readily forthcoming in the early-1980s. Thus, for example, uncertainty about the scale and feasibility of tourism in urban areas was one of the reasons for the commissioning by Merseyside Metropolitan Council of a tourism impact study in 1985 (DRV Research, 1986). One of its prime objectives was advocacy and the demonstration to the European Commission that tourism in Merseyside, and its associated economic impacts, were already significant and that, therefore, regeneration though tourism was a feasible option.

As an example of the results, it was estimated through the study that tourism's contribution to the Merseyside economy in 1985 was 12,000 direct jobs. In this context direct jobs were those in the businesses in which visitors spent their money. This was equivalent to the number of jobs in the chemical industry or mechanical engineering at that time.

Impacts by Type of Tourist

Tourists can be classified according either to the motivation for their visit, for example cultural visitors, or according to some aspect of their stay, for example their accommodation, their method of transport, their length of stay and so on. Culture has been one of the main themes of the attempt by city authorities to develop a tourism product. These attempts have focused on

museums and art galleries, the live performing arts and festivals
of the arts.

Table 9.2: The Impact of Cultural Visitors to Merseyside, 1985

Type of Impact	Classification of Impact		
	Primary	Secondary	Total
Spending (£m)	1.8	31.0	32.8
Income (£m)	0.8	4.3	5.1
Jobs (00's)	2.0	18.0	21.0

Source: Myerscough, 1988

As an example of the impacts of these cultural tourists, Table 9.2
has been calculated by Myerscough (1988) and relates to
Merseyside in 1985. This table is based on day and overnight visitors to Merseyside who attended museums, galleries and live
performing arts events. The values given have been adjusted to
reflect the differing level of the 'pull' of cultural opportunities in
the decision to visit Merseyside. The primary impacts cover the
economic benefits derived through the cultural organisation
(and the indirect and induced multiplier effects). The secondary
impacts cover the additional economic benefits as cultural visitors made use of other opportunities in Merseyside (accommodation, shops, etc, and the indirect and induced impacts of
spending in such businesses).

While Table 9.2 demonstrates the scale of cultural tourism's
impact on Merseyside in 1985, its importance can be judged by
the fact that the job figure is approximately half that for ship-
building at that time and one sixth of the overall estimate for
tourism in Merseyside in general. Of more importance, however,
in terms of evaluating the effectiveness of cultural tourism's contribution, is that the secondary impacts are significantly larger
than the primary impacts and, therefore, need to be included to
give a true picture of the impact.

THE IMPACTS OF PROJECTS

This section of the chapter is based upon a research study (Polytechnic of Central London *et al*, 1990) on tourism projects that had been supported by inner city grants. Thus the projects had been in receipt of either Urban Development Grants (UDG), Urban Programme Grants (UPG) or Derelict Land Grants (DLG).

Background

The results of three study projects are presented here: Hull Marina, Hull Post House and the Albert Dock in Liverpool. Basic details of these projects are given in Table 9.3. It should be noted that the costs of the project should be treated with care as the projects developed over a number of years and may have involved other financial sources not included in the value presented in the table. In addition, the Albert Dock complex is not all related to tourism as there are offices and residential properties incorporated within the development. The estimated cost for the tourism elements of the Albert Dock at that time was £17.8 million.

Table 9.3: The Selected Projects

Project	Current tourism related use	Former use	Site area	Total cost	Inner city grant	Type of grant
			Ha	£m	£m	
Hull Marina	Marina	Dock basin	4.9	3.9	2.8	DLG, UPG
Hull Post House	Hotel	Warehousing	1.4	5.6	1.6	UDG
Albert Dock	Shopping	Warehouses, museum, gallery, docks	13.0	62.7	43.0	UPG, UDG

On the basis of interviews and documentary evidence the three projects were assessed in terms of additionality and displacement. Each project was assessed as having complete additionality (would not have proceeded without the inner city grant) and only the Post House was assessed as having any displacement effect (and in that case it would have been marginal in terms of taking trade from elsewhere in the city).

The Total Impacts

The total impacts of the projects are made up of the primary and the secondary impacts (see Table 9.4). The primary impacts are those that result from the projects directly, either as a result of the construction phase or the operational phase. The analysis presented here focuses only on the operational phase and is, therefore, based on the spending by visitors. The primary impacts exclude any spending by residents of the city. The secondary impacts are the result of visitors to the projects (excluding city residents) spending money outside the development. The estimates should be treated with care due to the nature of the information used. For a detailed explanation please refer to the report (Polytechnic of Central London *et al*, 1990).

Table 9.4: The Primary and Secondary Impacts of Selected Projects

Type of Impact	Development		
	Albert Dock	Hull Post House	Hull Marina
Primary spend (£m)	3.4	*	*
Secondary spend (£m)	7.7	0.5	0.8
Total spend (£m)	11.1	*	*
Primary jobs	460 (274 FTE)	80 (70 FTE)	14 (10 FTE)
Secondary jobs	285 (179 FTE)	6 (4 FTE)	26 (20 FTE)
Total jobs	745 (453 FTE)	86 (74 FTE)	40 (30 FTE)
*	Not available for confidentiality reasons.		
FTE	Full-time, all-year equivalents.		

Source: Polytechnic of Central London *et al*, 1990

The results for each project have had the secondary impacts adjusted to reflect the importance of the project as a motivator for the visit. The trade creation element of the projects were: 60 per cent of the secondary spending for Albert Dock, 25 per cent of the secondary spending for the Post House and for the Marina, 75 per cent of the secondary spending for permanent berth holders and 88 per cent of the secondary spending for temporary berth holders. These adjustments for trade creation are reflected in the estimates of the number of jobs but not in the spending values.

The Nature of the Economic Impacts

As with the results for the cultural tourist on Merseyside, the above information about the economic impacts of the projects leaves a number of questions unanswered. These questions refer to the 'quality' of the impacts for the city and consist of three conditional factors once the scale of the impacts has been demonstrated.

Where Spending Takes Place

Table 9.5 provides information about the average amount spent per 24 hours by visitors to the different types of development. There are a number of aspects of this table that need explaining to prevent misunderstanding. First, the figures are for average spend. Thus there is a high spend figure at the Post House because it is not possible to stay there without spending money. Second, the berth holders spending at the Marina is based on the fee (annual for berth holders and last visit by visitors) converted to a per person per 24 hour figure (fee divided by the multiplication of the number of visits, the length of stay on the last visit and the number of people on last visit). Finally, the 'other' spend by berth holders is primarily (£19.88) on 'boat services' such as chandlery.

Table 9.5: The Spending per 24 hours by Visitors to the Selected Projects

Type of Spending	Development		
	Albert Dock	Hull Post House Berth holder	Hull Marina Visitors
	£ £	£	£
At development	3.65 63.35	12.64	2.08
Outside development:			
Accommodation	0.61 0.00	0.46	0.20
Food etc.	2.38 5.89	5.51	6.85
Shops	1.52 1.87	2.59	2.85
Leisure	0.45 0.21	0.23	0.13
Other	2.73 5.64	23.93	3.57
Total	11.34 76.96	45.36	15.68

Source: Polytechnic of Central London *et al*, 1990

Table 9.5 demonstrates that the impact of visitor spending is spread throughout the business community and is not confined to, or even primarily contained within, the development. Thus tourism type developments will contribute to the viability of other businesses through the spending of visitors.

Project Quality

Concern exists as to the quality of the jobs being created and the potential mismatch between the jobs that are being lost (have been lost) and the jobs that are being created. However, this concern with the quality of jobs may be misleading and may be based on stereotypes. To illustrate why this may be the case, Table 9.6 provides details of the types of jobs created at the three developments.

Table 9.6: The Types of Jobs at the Selected Projects

Type of Job	Development		
	Albert Dock	Hull Post House	Hull Marina
	%	%	%
All year *full-time*	36	85	57
part-time	40	4	21
Part-year *full-time*	10	11	0
part-time	13	0	21
Total	100	100	100
Full-time, all-year			
Male	35	42	55
Female	13	54	18
Part-time, all-year			
Male	9	1	27
Female	43	3	0
Total	100	100	100
Number of jobs: all-year	352	71	11
part-year	107	9	3

Source: Polytechnic of Central London *et al*, 1990

The concern may be based on stereotypes because, in general, tourism is seen as not providing real jobs because the jobs it does create are perceived as being primarily for women, part-time and seasonal. The concern is that such a pattern would not match the loss of jobs in, for example, manufacturing. However, as Table 9.6 demonstrates, there is no consistent pattern to the three developments studied and the patterns that are evident may not mirror the patterns of tourism employment found in areas that are more traditionally tourist based.

1. The highest level of seasonal employment is 23 per cent (Albert Dock) whilst the lowest is 11 per cent (Hull Post House).

2. The highest level of all year part-time employment is 53 per cent (Albert Dock) whilst the lowest is 4 per cent (Hull Post House).

3. The highest level of all year female employment is 57 per cent (Hull Post House) whilst the lowest is 18 per cent (Hull Marina).

Finally, at the Post House Hotel and at the Marina 40 per cent and 36 per cent of the jobs created respectively were 'white collar' (there is no comparable information for Albert Dock). This leaves 60 per cent and 54 per cent respectively that are manual. This can be viewed on the one hand as confirming that tourism offers mainly 'menial' jobs, whilst on the other, it could confirm that the developments are offering manual jobs at a time when other sectors are not and that, therefore, they are offering jobs which are appropriate to the inner city labour market.

One of the aims of urban policy is to improve the job prospects and opportunities of inner city residents. The above characteristics may suggest that the picture is not as bleak as some might suggest in terms of the match with the labour market. However, the final issue is that the critics may have missed the point. The alternative may not have been between tourism jobs and 'better' jobs but between tourism jobs and no jobs. In addition, as mentioned earlier the tourism developments may be having a 'soft economic' effect of improving the physical and perceptual environment and thereby increasing the prospects of alternative employment.

Cost of Creating Tourism

The third conditioning factor is whether tourism is 'better' value than the alternatives. Thus there is a call for comparative information on the cost of creating tourism-related jobs and jobs in other activities. Table 9.7 presents the cost of an unstandardised job (treating all jobs as equal) and of a standardised job (converting all jobs into all-year full-time equivalents) at each of the three projects. The table also provides that information for jobs at the project (primary jobs) and all jobs (primary and secondary jobs). The importance of taking account of the secondary impacts of tourism is evident in the table given the reduction in the cost per job when all jobs are included rather than simply those jobs at the project.

However, the cost per job figures may not be all that they

seem and finding comparable data for alternative activities is more difficult than might be expected. The main reasons for this are that:

a) the problems in identifying exactly how much has been spent at individual projects due to the time scales and variety of organisations involved;

b) the projects themselves may have objectives that are not related to job creation. For example, the creation of the Marina was as much about inducing property and land improvement in the area as with the actual creation of jobs;

c) whilst studies have been conducted on the costs per job of other activities the procedures involved, and the objectives of the alternative developments, may not allow direct comparisons.

Table 9.7: The Cost per Job Resulting from each of the Selected Projects

Type of Job	Development Grant cost per job (£000's)		
	Albert Dock	Hull Post House	Hull Marina
Primary			
Unstandardised	22.9	20.3	200.7
Standardised	38.3	22.5	286.7
All			
Unstandardised	13.6	16.9	70.3
Standardised	22.8	20.3	94.3

Source: Polytechnic of Central London *et al*, 1990

The conclusion presented in the Polytechnic of Central London report (1990), which drew on wider evidence than the three projects reported on here, was that tourism projects which did not have other primary objectives were at the low to middle end of the cost per job range. This conclusion was reached through a comparison with the costs of non-tourism projects (for example refurbished industrial units and managed units) as found in other studies and which ranged on average from £4,000 to £33,000. However, in addition it was concluded that while tourism projects generated jobs at a similar cost to other types of project they also generated a package of benefits (image, environment and local facility improvements) which other alternatives may not.

CONCLUSION

This chapter has demonstrated that tourism can have a significant economic impact on major urban areas. The chapter has concentrated on those impacts that are the result of, and include, the spending by visitors. However, it was also noted that tourism has other impacts on the environment (physical and social) which should not be underestimated, although they are in many ways more difficult to measure. For example, one of the major impacts of tourism development may be simply to change people's attitudes towards the area. Such changes may, in the long-term, prove as important as, if not more important than, the economic impacts documented in this chapter and which are the initial reasons put forward for public sector involvement in developing urban tourism. However, tourism is only one of a number of opportunities for regeneration. It can contribute in a number of ways but it cannot completely replace other economic activities.

REFERENCES

DRV Research: (1986) "An Economic Impact Study of Tourist and Associated Arts Development in Merseyside - The Overview Study" (DRV Research, Bournemouth).

C Law: (1994) *Urban Tourism - Attracting Visitors to Large Cities*, (Mansell, London).

Myerscough J: (1988) "The Economic Importance of the Arts in Merseyside" (Policy Studies Institute, London).

Polytechnic of Central London *et al:* (1990) "Tourism and the Inner City - An Evaluation of the Impact of Grant Assisted Tourism Projects" (HMSO, London).

Vaughan D R: (1977) "The Economic Impact of the Edinburgh Festival, 1976" (Scottish Tourist Board, Edinburgh) 1977.